LET'S

PREVENT DEPRESSION

AND ELIMINATE "HARMFUL"

MOOD SWINGS

Other Books by PAMELA ANNE MACCABEE

ATTENTION EXCHANGE
Copyright © 1977 by Pamela Anne Maccabee
Registration Number: A-859885

LET'S PRACTICE LOVING POLITICS
Using Emotion to Think Clearly and Deepen
Compassion
Copyright © 2015 by Pamela Anne Maccabee
ISBN-13: 978-1512237290
ISBN-10: 1512237299

THE WALKER BIOGRAPHIES—Shirley
Her Precious Birth, Her Education in Human Behavior,
Her Practice of Mindfulness and Skillful Emotionality,
and Her VERY First Most Amazing Assignment
Copyright © 2016 by Pamela Anne Maccabee
ISBN-13: 978-1523319855
ISBN-10: 1523319852

Let's
Prevent
Depression
and Eliminate
"Harmful" Mood Swings

THE STRESS-BUSTING PRACTICE
CALLED
SKILLFUL EMOTIONALITY

Dedication

To all my kindred spirits who deserve liberation from stress and stress-induced depression and mood swings.

With gratitude and love, to my dearest friend, Nancy Lee Pettit—she deserved far more from me than she ever received.

With deep appreciation and delight, to dear friend Kathleen Anne Garlington, animal lover and rescuer, musician, artist, humorist, and humanitarian.

Also, to my brother, Bruce Sargent Maccabee, to his wife, Jan Marie Pheneger Maccabee, to my loving mom, Bernice Frances Sargent Maccabee, to whom I am gratefully indebted, and to my dad Earl Philbrick Maccabee, whose one sacrifice made all the difference in my life.

To my nieces, Vanessa Niemann and Marie Frances Maccabee, and to my nephew, Ashley Philbrick Maccabee.

To my friend, John Ditman, who edited half the book, and my friend, Wesley Rawlings Cantwell, who has provided reassurance, encouragement, and inspiration.

To Violet Schamberger, who introduced me to the practice that has saved and enriched my life since 1974.

Something that we <u>all</u> once did automatically and effortlessly in order to feel better and reduce stress we were persuaded NOT to do except under certain circumstances.

Most of us got the message.   We learned not to do **_IT_** even though some of us needed to be able to do **_IT_** in order to stay healthy and happy.

For us **_IT_** had worked so well.

Now we need it _IT_ back.   We realize that OUR CHLDREN OF ALL AGES DESPERATELY NEED _IT_, too.!

We <u>all</u> need to reduce stress quickly so that we can be more relaxed, feel good about ourselves, enjoy warm and loving relationships, refresh and re-energize ourselves as needed, and think more quickly and clearly.   This means that we absolutely must relearn how and when to do **_IT_**

intentionally, thoughtfully, and skillfully.

We must let our children and young people do **_IT_**, too.

We all can do that,

TOGETHER.

TABLE OF CONTENTS

PART ONE—THE *SECRET* PROCESS: SECTION ONE

PART TWO—SELF-EXAMINATION 125

PART THREE—THE PRACTICE 135
OF SKILLFUL EMOTIONALITY

PART FOUR—THE PROCESS: 209
SECTION TWO

PART FIVE—BEING HIGH   **240**

BIOGRAPHICAL SUMMARY   288

RECOMMENDED READING   289

Preface

Depression and mood swings are not only a quality of life matter, these states of mind and spirit are a life-and-death matter, as you already know. Because of that I write this book which I hope will give you much more than hope—instead, an answer that just might work for you.

I had my long period of homicidal ideation with failed final preparation (thank goodness), I had my short period of suicidal ideation with one failure (thank goodness), and I can tell you this: none of us should have to give up our lives, or take the lives of others and then our own, because of any state of mind/emotion. It is not necessary, and I intend to explain why.

I am intolerably fortunate. As I say further on, I seem to be the luckiest person that I have ever met and talked openly with. Therefore, I am eagerly acting on my remaining obsession: sharing what I learned about preventing depression and eliminating "harmful" mood swings.

I once heard someone say, "We all have precious knowledge to share with one another." At the time that I heard that statement I was twenty-nine years old, still coming to terms with having had a complete and nearly fatal psychological collapse when I was twenty-three. It had turned me inside out and my life upside down, and I hoped the statement was true because believing it made me feel a little better about myself; maybe I'd eventually figure out what <u>my</u> *precious knowledge to share* was going to be.   Well, forty-plus years later, I obviously am convinced the statement is true (this book is the evidence).

I believe that you have precious knowledge to share, also, so, I will be patiently waiting for you to uncover and in your own time share <u>your</u> *precious knowledge.* Meanwhile, by reading this book you will find out what I discovered— the lightning-fast <u>totally natural</u> stress-buster that saved and changed my life.

What's really strange is, I didn't have to look far to find this stress-buster; it was with me all the time.   I just didn't recognize it.   It's with you, too.   You will see what I mean.   When you are ready to hear what it is, I will eagerly tell you.   Until then, please, proceed with patience and determination.   Yes, jump ahead if you like, but if you instantly doubt what I will be telling you, please make sure that you read Part One, at least.

Thank you.

> *Expect the unexpected and all will be well.*
> Lilly the Cat

INTRODUCTION

What did I discover? This: we are born possessing a natural physiological process that at any given time can rapidly reduce, and even eliminate, stress (feelings of tension, pressure, and strain). At the beginning of this book I referred to it and named it, ***IT***.

IT is a stress-busting physiological process as natural as breathing. Although everyone thinks they know all about it, ***IT*** is misunderstood. It gets little to no respect from most adults who suspect it is either useless, an indulgence, or harmful; those adults who admit to its value are, nevertheless, extremely hesitant to use it because very few of their family, friends, and acquaintances expect them to. It certainly gets little recognition from the scientific community despite all that it does for us and would do, if we were to let it. Fortunately, there is some good news. Now, at least, we know some of the reasons why it enables us to feel more relaxed and optimistic (explanation to follow). Despite the paucity of scientific evidence for its truly enormous and uninvestigated value, personal experiences like mine should be persuasive.

This process is so ordinary that few know to give it credit for anything. In fact, people usually feel it is something to be *gotten over* (endured or survived) rather than something to be encouraged, promoted, and used like a tool for happy, rational, health-full living.

1

Because we are often judged and criticized for *allowing* **IT** to occur hardly any of us are comfortable with the process, and some of us are downright afraid of it.   As a result, we usually can't take advantage of its impressive stress-busting capabilities and we typically make it difficult for others to utilize it even when it obviously would be beneficial for them to do so, which IS tragic.

This process saves lives.   Yes, I just said that—*saves lives*!

The use of this process is our birthright.   I hope to not only reacquaint you with it but persuade you to experience this process for yourself, not once but multiple times. Only then can you learn if it will do for you what it has done for me which is <u>EVERYTHING</u>.

Believe me, you have been deprived of *ITs* use for far too long. <u>Together, let's change that!</u>

THE PRELIMINARIES

Note: actually, this is not a book.

This is a conversation.

Do not forget!

THIS

IS

A

CONVERSATION!

SOMEHOW I HOPE TO HEAR FROM YOU.

CHAPTER 1

LET ME PERSUADE YOU

This book is a heartfelt exercise in persuasion. It will cover, not necessarily in this order:

1. the practice of *skillful emotionality* and its immediate and long term benefits.
2. the stress-busting process that I have already referred to as **IT**.
3. our need to retrain our brains so that we can again employ this process successfully.
4. the viewpoint that we all need to gradually adopt regarding the process's importance as it is attitude and viewpoint that will determine whether or not any of us use the process and benefit fully from it.
5. the importance of including other stress-reduction practices such as meditation, prayer, exercise, etc., rather than depending on this natural practice alone.
6. a mini-questionnaire, sentence completion exam, and true-false test on your beliefs (attitudes, viewpoints, values) regarding the process—<u>by then you will know what the process is and you will be able to recognize the thinking that will prevent you from using it effectively and efficiently</u>.
7. deprogramming yourself (you will discover why deprogramming is absolutely necessary).

8. the difference between feeling feelings and experiencing the process and why this is important to understand.
9. the simple *skills* that will help you *allow* as well as intentionally activate this process only at the time and place of your own choosing (most *skills* are familiar and are easy to relearn and practice).
10. a little about stress and the science regarding this process (provided in case you hesitate to experiment with the process unless there is <u>some</u> apparent scientific justification to do so).
11. anecdotes illustrating how I use the process.
12. encouragement to obtain professional help and guidance for selecting professionals who respect the process.
13. a format that enables you, family, friends, and strangers to practice the *skills* together so that you, YOU, are in charge of your use of the process.

<u>*Working together*</u> **we all can prevent depression and eliminate "harmful" mood swings.**

Skillful emotionality, whether we practice alone or with others, helps us become adept at allowing, activating, and when we wish, prolonging, this natural, supremely effective stress-busting process. *Skillful emotionality* is psychologically as well as physically therapeutic but it is not a form of professional *psychotherapy* that nonprofessionals have adapted for their own use. No.

One last thing: if at any point you become impatient with the rather slow pace of this book, please read Chapters 8, 9, 10, and 11 and then jump to the section on the practice of *skillful emotionality*.

This is your guide. Call it your Greenie, anything you like. You name it! It is for YOU.

PLEASE, READ THE ENTIRE TABLE OF CONTENTS.

CHAPTER 2

ARE YOU INCLUDED IN THE TARGET AUDIENCE?

The book's target audience is those of us who inherited a vulnerability to depression/mood swings. However, anyone alive on our dear Planet Earth can find value in what I share here because the focus is on stress which no one can totally avoid, especially since *good* things as well as undesirable things can trigger stress as well. If you are psychologically healthy and under stress because of illness or relationship/work problems or any other combination of problems which we will euphemistically refer to as *challenges*, the *process* and the practice of *skillful emotionality* can definitely work for you.

Actually, even if stress and depression/mood swings are totally unfamiliar to you, you, too, deserve to find out for yourself if *skillful emotionality* will help you make your life easier so that you can:

1. stay relatively relaxed and optimistic.
2. make helpful, constructive decisions rather than stress-driven unhelpful or destructive decisions.
3. neither give up nor give in because of stress <u>unless</u> it makes sense to do so.
4. save desirable relationships, jobs, and educational opportunities rather than lose them because of stress.

9

5. be able to feel contentment, happiness, fulfillment, and peace of mind on an ongoing basis and also, because of reduction in, or absence of, stress, be able to feel joy and gratitude for your friends, loved ones, and for Life itself.

Now, as I said, those of us who inherited vulnerability to depression/mood swings are the target audience. I think that we have a very special need to know about this process since stress is usually the major driver for our moods.   In fact, I like to be specific in this way: I inherited a vulnerability to <u>stress-induced</u> depression/mood swings and that is why a stress-busting process works so well for me.

Unless you have guessed what this process is, you may still be wondering, *what is it*?   Obviously, it involves emotion (or *skillful emotionality* is an absurd name for the practice).   Unfortunately, because I worry that you, like most of us, have learned to disregard (and discard as a foolish waste of time) this process, I must ask you to be gracious and patient and wait for ***THE BIG REVEAL***. As you read, just remember that the process is a life saver. If for forty-three years this process has enabled me to avoid depression and harmful mood swings through both difficult and delightful times, it's got to be good.

Forty-three years is pretty impressive track record, isn't it?!

I think so!!

CHAPTER 3

SHOULD THIS PROCESS BECOME YOUR ONLY HEALTH PRACTICE?

Good grief, no. I hope not! You are such a marvelously complex being possessing a brain that may forever defy our efforts to understand its full complexity, including its potential to *serve* us mentally/intellectually, emotionally, physically, and spiritually, that it would be a genuine pity if you failed to take advantage of a full range of healthful practices. Yes, this stress-busting process is totally natural and I hope you will embrace it as I have, but it must never be your only one!. We evolved (or were designed) to make extensive use of it (and I do mean extensive), but the only health practice? Look at me! Over the years, I have enriched and saved my life by:

1. reading fiction and nonfiction such as **Starship Troopers** by Robert Anson Heinlein, and by watching movies such as the 1971 action/drama film, **Billy Jack**, the second in a film quadrilogy that was written, directed, and produced by Tom Laughlin (Thomas Robert Laughlin Jr.) and Delores Taylor, both of whom also starred in three of the **Billy Jack** movies; they are deceased and revered by me. .

2. doing creative writing as well as *reflective journaling* which is an extremely useful discipline

where we not only report or describe in detail incidents and situations that occur or thoughts and memories that arise, but analyze the experiences/thoughts/memories by asking ourselves questions that occur to us as we write—what's really important, what do we believe *really* happened, how did *it* make us feel, how did *it* affect what we did and will do, could we have done things differently, why are we thinking what we are thinking, how are our thoughts, beliefs, attitudes, and values influencing what we do, what does *it* mean to us, etc.

3. meditating (for years intermittently until in 2016 when I found a group with whom to meditate — only once a week, I confess, but wow).

4. praying (got me through college thanks to InterVarsity Christian fellowship, my first year of teaching, out of a psychiatric hospital, and through the next two and a half years of recovery).

5. running and also cardio-karate, which offered the best workout I ever had.   (During hour-long cardio-karate workouts I learned not to fear perspiring.   Imagine, fearing perspiring!!)

6. *exercycling* (stationary bike, a Tunturi, that I truly loved) from 1978 to 2010 while talking on the phone, listening to music, reading books, watching movies, studying textbooks, and practicing skillful emotionality alone and with phone companions.

7. mountain biking.
8. peer counseling.
9. intermittently practicing simple yoga (I may do simple yoga stretches *tonight* as I am as stiff as hardened concrete).

All the above are <u>healthful</u> activities, obviously. For you, I listed them so that they would really stand out.

When you are able, try to expand your own dependable stress-busting toolkit...and I hope that yours will soon include the totally relaxing, yet paradoxically energizing, practice of *skillful emotionality.*

CHAPTER 4

A LITTLE BIT ABOUT ME...*I HAD NO IDEA*

As I said, I have been unusually lucky. I actually believe that I am the luckiest person that I have ever met. Is that possible?

I am lucky because I learned how to intelligently use this most rapid-acting, stress-busting physiological process that humanity naturally possesses. I use it like an expert, in fact, even use it brilliantly—I can reduce even eliminate stress and feel better (or good or terrific) <u>in less than one minute</u>. You deserve to know how I do that especially since I believe that you will be able to do the same.

I didn't learn to use the process from choice, incidentally. Oh, no! I learned to use it because some unexpected things happened in my life. (I am sure that you could say the same for yourself, at least as regards to *unexpected things* happening.)

Unexpected developments really are the norm, aren't they. I had no idea how things would work out after mine occurred. I was twenty-one when I began my first year of teaching sixth graders in Glastonbury, Connecticut, USA—that was September, 1966. I had no idea that my dad would die March, 1967, and March, 1968, I would end up on a general hospital psych unit for a month receiving electro-convulsive therapy because I had been high and

14

planning to execute a very dangerous childhood fantasy which had developed after I saw my brother punished so severely that our mom screamed, "Stop, you're going to kill him." (Long after my hospitalization my mom told me about this incident. Perhaps she was hoping to find out if I remembered what had happened; I didn't, in fact, not for decades.)

Of course, each one of us was traumatized by that experience of violence and responded to it in our own way. Sadly, we knew nothing about the value of this simple, natural process that I love and therefore the deep loving relationships that we could have had never materialized, a familiar story I am sure. If only we had known that the process which has saved my life could have saved our family, too.

My dad was a thoroughly good and kind person. I suspect that he had been drinking alcohol when he beat my brother because, in the 1990's, my brother told me that he had been "an alcoholic." (That was news to me!)

In my dad's defense, I want you to know that he had received beatings from his dad, who probably had, also, from his dad. Since alcohol likely was involved, my dad's behavior makes sense: possibly, stress of being a parent, low frustration tolerance, little impulse control, and what is called *restimulation* and...explosion. I am certain that when he became sober he was horrified by what he had done to my brother.

Now, we are going to backtrack to my general hospital psychiatric unit experience...the childhood fantasy referred to above, which in a modified state had endured for well over fifteen years, was quickly eliminated by the 1968 course of twelve ECT. Although it had a disastrous effect on my ability to learn new information and therefore was terribly demoralizing, it worked. I am positive that medication would not have eliminated my dangerous obsession fast enough. (Current recipients of ECT are invited to share their experiences with it on what I hope will eventually be a Facebook page for this book.).

April 23, 1968, I was discharged from the general hospital psychiatric unit. Following only a few weeks at home, I returned to my sixth grade class to finish out the school year. Really, I was zombie, a place holder, only. I never should have been there. (My psychiatrist later admitted his error in encouraging my return. It was his *get back on the horse* theory, or so he told me. He <u>was</u> wise about the ECT, fortunately.)

More *no ideas*. I had no idea that once that second teaching year had ended I next would survive a scary nearly fatal (for someone else) summer, teach for four days of my third year of teaching, attempt suicide, spend eight months in Vermont's only state hospital, be

16

discharged to live in a half-way house for six weeks, volunteer with a Girls Scout Troop, get an apt, and finally, in August or September 1969, filled with dread and psychoactive medication, start a genuinely new independent working life in the kitchen of a local hospital.

Incidentally, I would have refused to leave the hospital if my psychiatrist had not promised me that I could return and live there if things didn't work out. I knew people who lived there and to me they seemed quite happy and relaxed, the result of medication, of course. At that time I was extremely ignorant as to the effects of the psychoactive medications in use.

Although I never returned to teaching, because of the kindness of a great number of people who over the next five years hired me in spite of the psychiatric history—I was afraid to lie about it—my life has been uphill in the best, <u>ascending</u>, sense.

You need to know that there were quite a few more things about which I had no idea. For example, I had no idea that eventually my mom, who wanted to console me (I felt like the family failure), would tell me that apparently I had inherited a vulnerability. From the following list you can guess what that vulnerability is—

●my mom (black dog depression, intermittent and fleeting, kept a secret until after my hospitalization).

17

•her mom (depression).

•my dad (seasonal affective disorder with mood swings).

•one of his cousins (depression).

•one of his uncles (depression).

•one of my cousins (depression)

•one of my second cousins (depression)

•two other related individuals (depression and/or mood swings).

As far as I know, only four of my relatives sought professional help. I was one of them. As far as I know, only two of them attempted suicide. One of them was me. However, I am not going to tell you that suicide has not been considered, often, by some of those I will not mention. (I am not referring to myself here.)

I mentioned having *no idea* about a lot of things There is one more thing about which I had no idea...that in 1974 a friend would introduce me to a peer counseling program that taught participants how to restore their ability to make intelligent use of this as-of-yet unnamed process. Fortunate me! A delusion that at the time I was paying attention to, which was altruistic in nature but definitely unrealistic and potentially destabilizing, completely lost its appeal after one experience with this natural process that I so highly recommend, and learning to understand

and utilize that process was the beginning of <u>my</u> liberation from depression/mood swings.

Presently, I most want you to know that everything you read here about *skillful emotionality* is based entirely on my various and valuable experiences with that peer counseling program. Further on, I tell you about that life-changing first experience with the peer counseling program and with the process it extols.

I have been exceptionally lucky. I really do hope that what I share with you in this book will make you lucky, too.

CHAPTER 5

TIME FOR *TRUE CONFESSIONS*: THIS IS A DEPROGRAMMING AND BRAIN RETRAINING MANUAL <u>JUST FOR YOU</u>

From your childhood you have been so completely programmed to distrust/mistrust this process, to deeply doubt yourself because of the desire to use it, and to feel bewildered, worthless, unwanted, and judged by others if you *allow* it to occur, that after discovering what the process is you might slam this book down on the nearest table or floor while growling to yourself, "Ridiculous. Absurd!   It can't *do* all that!"

I am not imagining that you may react like that; I predict it.   I frequently get that reaction from those who are suffering from prolonged stress, and here is a response that really saddens me: "Maybe it's good for some people but it's not for me.   I know myself!"   Those who hold this belief are unable to even imagine that the process could help them.

Because I don't want you to miss out on something that could have a phenomenally positive impact on your life, I intend to help you disabuse yourself of the most erroneous belief about this process—that it has really limited value.

Once you realize it has <u>unlimited</u> value you can with determination begin your own deprogramming.

So, this is **YOUR** deprogramming manual. Get ready for—

repetition of ideas, repetition of ideas and repetition of ideas, repetition of ideas, and repetition of ideas, repetition of ideas! HAD ENOUGH?

Expect repetition of almost anything, including ideas, because this deprogramming manual must be used precisely as that. <u>You really do **HAVE** to retrain your brain</u>, and you can! I know that you can.

EXPECT REPETITION BECAUSE THIS IS ESSENTIAL INFORMATION. THAT IS MY OPINION!!

Yes, I believe that knowledge about this process is essential. Does it matter if only a few of us reclaim our birthright process, or instead, if millions of us reclaim it? I say, it REALLY matters. This is what I think: at least here in the United States of America, for a wide variety of reasons that are social and economic, despite one of the highest standards of living on Planet Earth if not the highest, unbearable stress and depression are nearly an epidemic.   Incidence of suicide has increased for all ages, including for our young.   In fact, according to an April 22, 2016, headline from The New York Times, the "U.S. Suicide Rate Surges to a 30-Year High."

For information on anxiety and depression experienced by United States children and teenagers, I highly recommend the website of the Centers for Disease Control and Prevention on child and teenage depression. https://www.cdc.gov/childrensmentalhealth/depression.ht ml.

What about depression in the United Kingdom (UK), you ask.   September 19,2017, Denis Campbell, Health Policy Editor at The Guardian newspaper, reported on a government-funded study of the mental health of young citizens which was conducted by academics from University College London and the University of Liverpool.   The results were based on responses of over 10,000 young people age fourteen.   Shockingly, 24% of girls fourteen and 9% of boys, same age, responding to a questionnaire, selected responses exposing depression. Cited as sources of stress and pressure were: "stress at school, body image issues, bullying, and the pressure created by social media."   That is a quote from Marc

Bush, chief policy adviser at a the charity, Young Minds. He referred, also, to "bereavement, domestic violence, and neglect."

Parents, who also filled out questionnaires for this study, were inaccurate in their assessments of their young people's mental states. If you wonder how that is possible, you will probably have your answers before you get very far in this book. I was a depressed child and no one knew it, including me...and what that depression lead to was not at all good because the fruits of depression are always rotten.

Are they always rotten? Those of us who sincerely believe that we could not be creative without the experience of depression are creative in spite of depression, not because of it. Depression is not necessary! You will discover why I make this claim.

Stress-busting ability, gradually perfected by all humans, is a rational objective. Worldwide, the challenges facing each of us and our entire species will never diminish, will instead increase. Unending stress will become the norm for more and more of us and stress without respite leads to hopelessness and despair as well as unwanted physical conditions, disorders, and diseases, in short, to SUFFERING ON A VAST SCALE!

Unending stress will also lead to increased incidents of violence and terrorism here in the United States and worldwide because desperate and deprived people do desperate things that they otherwise would not do if their lives included safety, security, and all of the necessities of physical, psychological, and spiritual well-being.

We must face it—unending stress will maintain the cycle of irrational decision-making by those politicians and behind-the-scenes individuals who <u>really</u> are in charge of humanity's future (we won't name names, will we). If you are one of these individuals and you are reading this book, I beg you, "Keep reading. Just keep reading." You may hold the monetary and governmental key to humanity's rescue and Earth's salvation.

So, seriously, are you somewhat ready for **The Big Reveal**? I do hope so. It's coming up shortly, but I don't know if you are ready for it yet.

Perhaps not.

CHAPTER 6

STRESS AND THE *SECRET* PROCESS

You probably know about stress already, but I feel compelled to remind us both (you and me) that no one who lives can escape stress. From before birth (meaning in the womb) until death it is present in our lives producing mental or bodily tension which we may or may not consciously experience as pressure and strain.

Sources of stress can be external, i.e., environmental, social, or situational, and internal, i.e., psychological, physical, and for example, from responses to medical procedures and medication. Dysfunction of any kind puts us under stress. Harmful levels of stress and/or prolonged unmanaged stress place all of us at risk of myriad physical and psychological problems, problems that may take years, or seconds, to develop or become evident.

I am not providing you with a list of stress-related problems, ailments, and illnesses, as well as harmful behavioral responses to stress, because to me the list would be informative but horrifying: every organ and system, from brain to skin to joints to heart to colon to endocrine and digestive systems, is negatively affected by stress (and our inability to relieve it) due to our body's stress-responses which are meant to protect us but can cause permanent and ultimately fatal damage.

Because of the potential damage that can result from unalleviated, unmanageable stress, your stress-busting toolkit should never be empty.   Further on in the book I briefly bring your attention to the **proven value of meditation** among others not mentioned, but for now I want you to contemplate the following:

there REALLY is one totally natural stress-busting process that is hardly ever mentioned.   It is the one you will read about here.

CHAPTER 7

THE *SECRET* PROCESS AND YOUR SOCIAL PROGRAMING

Starting with the moment you were born, whenever you were under stress (physical, psychological), your body effortlessly and automatically activated the vital and totally natural stress-reducing physiological process that I refuse to name until **THE BIG REVEAL**. This complex (electrobiochemical) process which adults assumed was of limited value occurred even if you were unaware of any tension, pain, or emotional distress. (Conscious awareness of tension, pain, or emotional pain was never necessary for this process to work like a charm.)

Once the process was completed, you felt refreshed and relaxed. If very young you may have fallen asleep or smiled at any humans near you and contentedly engaged with them. If older and mobile, you probably bounced off to do whatever you wanted to do as long as it was *permissible*, of course...mmmm...well...

As you grew older, you became programmed by society to inhibit the process's activation except in certain situations. The programming was intentional though not malicious and it was quite simple: either you were told not to do **IT** or, because you were naturally super aware of and supersensitive to facial expressions, if you saw disapproval or discomfort on the faces of those around you when you tried to use the process you instantly squelched or suppressed it.

That programming was more than unfortunate. Its use would have helped you reduce stress and manage your moods and emotions on a daily basis so that depression and mood swings were avoided as you proceeded from childhood into the teen and young adult years. Without the process, you gradually found other ways, possibly some of them harmful, to deal with stress and with your emotions.

As an adult, you have learned to live without access to this lightning-fast stress-busting process and you probably have helped others to live without it, too. But really!!! Something so useful! Does it make sense to eliminate its use? No, no, no. no. Fight for yourself—retrain your brain and get it back, like I did!

PART ONE

THE *SECRET* PROCESS: SECTION ONE

Really,

you are not going to believe

what the secret process is.

Trust me,

you won't.

A most humble process

will enrich us all—

physically, mentally/intellectually, emotionally, and spiritually.

CHAPTER 8

THE BIG REVEAL AND DEPROGRAMMING #1

So, what is the as-of-yet unnamed process, this something that we all once did automatically and effortlessly in order to feel better and reduce stress but were persuaded NOT to do, this something that we learned not to do even though some of us (like me) needed to be able to do it in order to stay healthy and happy.

What is this *IT* that worked so well that I call it nearly magical? Why *should* we all want back? How did it help us reduce stress quickly, become more relaxed, feel better, and therefore think more clearly? Why do we have to re-learn how and when to do this *something* which we once did automatically and effortlessly, and why should we learn to do *IT* intentionally, thoughtfully, and skillfully?

What is this process that I revere and credit with my health and well-being because it enables me to:

- feel better in minutes (even less than a minute if I really concentrate).
- think with greater clarity.

- experience the goodness of life without the specter of depression and harmful mood swings constantly hovering over me.

GET READY!   BRACE YOURSELF!

BRACE

YOUR

SELF !

**The process is called *emotional discharge*
and**

it is this:

CRYING and/or LAUGHING A BIT, with Tears

Often, it is

CRYING and/or LAUGHING HARD, with TEARS

WARNING

BE ADVISED: EMOTIONAL DISCHARGE CAN UNEXPECTEDLY *UNLOCK* THOUGHTS/IDEAS, FEELINGS, EMOTIONS, AND MEMORIES THAT WE ARE NOT READY TO NOTICE (OR EXPERIENCE) AND CONSCIOUSLY THINK ABOUT.   SOMETIMES IT IS WISE TO CRY IN THE PRESENCE OF A SKILLED AND TRUSTED THERAPIST WHO HAS ALREADY STATED HIS OR HER CONFIDENCE THAT CRYING HAS VALUE.

Emotional discharge is *crying/laughing* when we experience love, awe, gratitude, joy, etc. Strong emotions such as these naturally trigger tears.

Emotional discharge also is *crying/laughing* due to irritation, frustration, anger, rage, sadness, grief, anguish, regret, remorse, bitterness, shame, helplessness, fear, terror, etc.

Emotional discharge is also crying/laughing as we think about our lives— past, present, and future; about our relationships with family and friends, humanity, and our beloved planet, Earth; about our faiths and philosophies of life; about politics and society; about fields of knowledge that we are so emotionally attached to that we can cry just contemplating them: science, math, technology, archeology, paleontology, astronomy, etc.

Emotional discharge is the dual-purpose demagnetizer that all humans are born to employ exactly like a tool because...

it erases BOTH stress and emotional pain big-time!

You probably won't believe me, of course. That is no surprise so please read the next chapter, *Some Science About This Awesome, Misunderstood Process.*

33

In the past, I would not have believed my statements about busting stress and reducing emotional pain; however, my experiences have proved the statement to be true, for me. If you are a human being, which I know you are, it just might prove to be true, for you, also . If you read further, you will learn exactly how you can *make it so*, for yourself.

ESSENTIAL INFORMATION

WHEN YOU PRACTICE *SKILLFUL EMOTIONALITY* YOU <u>INTEND</u> TO DISCHARGE EMOTION BECAUSE YOU WANT TO BUST STRESS.

<u>HOWEVER,</u>

<u>YOU DO NOT TRY</u> TO DISCHARGE EMOTION.

NO.

YOU USE SPECIFIC SKILLS DISCUSSED IN THIS BOOK, SKILLS WHICH HELP US ACTIVATE EMOTION SO THAT WE <u>CAN</u> BUST STRESS.

CHAPTER 9

SOME SCIENCE ABOUT THIS AWESOME, MISUNDERSTOOD PROCESS

From start to finish, birth till death, emotional discharge is meant to play an important stress-busting role in the lives of human beings. If we have received truly harmful-to-health programming, we are convinced that emotional discharge weakens us and impairs our ability to think clearly and tackle life's challenges with courage, but this viewpoint is dangerously wrong; instead, because of its ability to reduce and even eliminate stress, emotional discharge strengthens and empowers us and improves our ability to think clearly and act with *rational* courage.

Skeptical? Well, won't you at least finish reading this particular chapter as well as the following chapter on inflammation. Maybe there are a few things about emotional discharge that you will find encouraging.

If this is your own book, checkmark the familiar and perhaps cross out that which you strongly doubt.

☐ The positive effects of discharge are not imagined. Research proves discharge (at least laughing - will explain later) to be a stress-buster extraordinaire: it not only drives down stress, it reduces physical and emotional pain.

☐ Stress-and-emotion crying/laughing (*psychic tears*) removes the hormone ACTH from the body which is a REALLY good thing since when we are under stress this hormone stimulates the production of a notorious hormone called the stress hormone—cortisol. Although cortisol helps to prepare us for fight-or-flight, if it remains elevated in our bloodstream because stress fails to abate or our feeling of being under stress persists for any reason, the role it plays is definitely not positive. Elevated cortisol levels have a negative effect on learning and memory, our immune function, weight, blood pressure, cholesterol levels, and heart health Stress that is chronic is implicated in the increased risk for depression and other mental health problems, lower life expectancy, and especially for adolescents, lower psychological resilience.

☐ Psychic tears activate the production of extremely beneficial morphine-like substances called enkephalins such as leucine-enkephalin, and endorphins, both of which function like opium-based drugs, blocking the transmission of pain signals. Both also, in some way, make the pain that we feel as we discharge bearable, and both are produced whether or not we know *why* we are crying/laughing with tears. We do not have to seek—or gain—insight in order for us to receive genuine relief from stress and from emotional pain. **Remember this: insight is not necessary; <u>tears are.</u>**

Don't demand that you know <u>the why</u>

when you suddenly feel the urge—TO CRY.

☐ Because tears are so essential for the release of endorphins and leucine enkephalin, **we must consider tears *our goal*.** Successful practitioners of skillful emotionality never forget:

tears are not a step to a goal.
They *are* the goal.

☐ During emotional discharge we laugh often. Research indicates that laughter increases blood flow to the brain. In fact, laughter affects blood vessels throughout the body the same way aerobic exercise does, helping them function better. Researchers at the University of Maryland School of Medicine in Baltimore discovered that the endothelium, tissue that forms the inner lining of blood vessels, expands in order to increase blood flow during laughter. Mental stress reduces blood flow by causing constriction (vasoconstriction) of the endothelium of the blood vessels. Average blood flow increased 22% from a baseline reading during laughter and decreased 35% during mental stress. Why is that important to us? I have no doubt that crying produces the same beneficial results. Someday, there will be funding for research to prove this. Now, who reading these words will decide to develop a research program to test this assumption? You?

☐ Intriguing research was reported between October 2013 and February 2017, by the following: Time Magazine (October 2013); NPR Radio (October 2013); The Atlantic Magazine (February 2017); Live Science.com (Feb., 2017);), and others. Apparently, during sleep the brain shrinks. Why would it do that? There are several theories all dependent on the focus of the research. One theory may be of special interest to us, at this time. University of Rochester Medical Center researchers report that while we sleep the brain's neurons shrivel up by 60% as they remove waste/toxins and deposit it, through the recently identified *glymphatic system*, into cerebrospinal fluid where it is then is returned to the circulatory system (from whence it came) for disposal by the liver. Now, why is that theory of special interest to us? Because it is likely that the very same process occurs during discharge of emotion, with some toxins going into the cerebrospinal fluid and some into tears (See Dr. Maiken Nedergaard, Co-Director of the URMC Center for Translational Neuromedicine.) Now, AGAIN, who reading these words will decide to develop a research program to test this assumption? Will you?

CHAPTER 10

SOME SCIENCE—CAN INFLAMMATION CAUSE DEPRESSION?

As mentioned earlier, medical science has long accepted the fact that chronic physical and psychological stress causes chronic inflammation which can, over time, affect not only organs and systems in the body but also cause the body's immune system to malfunction. But due to stress can the brain suffer inflammation, also?

While web surfing today I accidentally encountered a research gold mine that you will get to cautiously explore further on. I say *cautiously* explore because the theories and interpretation of the data may and may not be totally or partially correct—my explanation for the data most definitely differs from theirs. You will see.

First, let's backtrack. Why not first take a look at some interesting older articles on the subject of stress and health. Apparently, stress, health, and the immune system became serious research topics because of the Apollo space flights of the 1960's and 1970's. NASA doctors realized that the astronauts' immune systems were being negatively affected by the stress the men were under.

Scientific research on the aforementioned topics has not in any way diminished over the years; for good reason, it has increased, and the articles that I have selected are simply the ones I easily located online...such as this one: in <u>1986</u>, Dr. Steven Locke, a Harvard Medical School professor at that time, and Douglas Colligan, a free-lance author, published the ground-breaking book, THE HEALER WITHIN which introduced the public to the totally new field of psychoneuroimmunology, a study of the ways that stress, emotions, and attitude:

1. affect both health and the treatment of illness.
2. seem to play a major role in the development of disorders and illness as well as in the course of recovery (or the reverse).
3. influence the strength and effectiveness of the immune system.

March 23, <u>2014</u>, Prevention Magazine provided an article written by Kate Lowenstein, "Is Inflammation What's Causing Your Depression?"   Among other things, her article focused on the work of Dr. Gary Kaplan, D.O., an osteopathic physician who then suspected (and still does) that brain inflammation is likely implicated in the development of depression.   His work with patients can be found in his book published in 2014 by Rodale Press: TOTAL RECOVERY.

He believes that microglia, extremely sensitive infection-fighting cells located throughout the brain and spinal cord which are a part of our immune system, become overactive due to chronic stress, producing inflammation.

He believes, also, that psychological and physical trauma that occurred early in life also can cause inflammation. Research supports this view: higher rates of inflammation are seen in adults whose childhoods were stressful and/or included physical or emotional trauma.

Posted January 8, 2017 on the "Psychology Today" Internet website, you will find this article written by Marlynn Wei M.D., J.D., "New Research Shows Depression Linked with Inflammation." Dr. Wei cites a recent study published in "The Journal of Clinical Psychiatry." Data was examined from 14, 275 people who between 2007 and 2012 were interviewed to screen for depression. Blood samples were taken. The results? Those suffering from depression had 46% higher levels of C-reactive protein (CRP), a marker for inflammatory disease, than non-depressed individuals. This builds on evidence that inflammation indeed plays some role in depression, and according to Dr. Wei, this raises the question that Dr. Kaplan considered: is depression a psychoneuroimmunological disorder?

From a June 21, 2017, posting by *MedicalXpress.com*, "Researchers Discover Brain Inflammation in People with OCD" (obsessive-compulsive disorder), we have a summary of a study published on this date in *JAMA*

Psychiatry.   Researchers used positron emission tomography (PET), a form of brain imaging, plus an adaptation that enabled them to effectively utilize a chemical dye, to measure the activity of the immune cells, the microglia, in brain areas already known to function differently in OCD sufferers.   In those brain areas inflammation was definitely higher than in the rest of the brain., 32% higher.   Significant?   Yes.

So...it looks as though the brain is under assault—by inflammation—and researchers studying depression, anxiety, and OCD as well as other disorders, are on the hunt (1) for the specific factors contributing to brain inflammation, and (2) for potential treatments, including use of anti-inflammatory drugs.   That is good.

BUT!

What if our poor suffering brains are simply reacting to our failure to reduce or eliminate stress using the emotional discharge process?   Science has proved that unrelieved stress causes inflammation that can occur anywhere in the body.   So...

Also, let's remind ourselves of the research that I referred to earlier involving sleep, the expulsion of waste material/neurotoxins from the brain, and their transport, by the glymphatic system, into the cerebrospinal fluid and ultimately out of the body. It makes sense to me that neurons unable to expel enough waste material (neurotoxins) could be compromised by inflammation. Of course, I speak as someone with a good imagination who is really quite ignorant.

IF depression actually is a psychoneuroimmunological disorder, one caused by chronic stress, isn't it likely that the emotional discharge process will have a positive impact on inflammation? I am opinionated; I believe so, and I believe this, also: although in the short term anti-inflammatory medicines might reliably alleviate symptoms of depression/mood swings, it is a regular practice of intentional emotional discharge when there is stress and strain that will reduce and possibly eliminate all brain inflammation in the best way possible—naturally.

If you are a professional with the appropriate credentials, won't you design and obtain funding for a study that at least examines the relationship between levels of C-reactive protein and frequency of emotional discharge? Really, think about it! How hard would it be to take pre-and-post-session blood samples from depressed and *high* volunteers who would meet three times a week with a therapist trained to help them *discharge emotion* (bust stress the natural way). How hard?

If you agree to do this, please let me know so that I can spread the word and also weep with gratitude. It appears that most people won't *dare try tears* unless there's undeniable proof that discharging emotion reduces physical and mental stress, so research results could play a major role in saving and enriching lives.

Finally, here are Dr. Wei's last thoughts on inflammation and how we can help ourselves reduce inflammation

1. reduce stress in your life as much as possible.
2. eat fewer inflammatory foods (she mentions fried foods, soda, white bread and pastries, margarine, lard, and red meat).
3. exercise regularly.
4. do mind-body exercises like yoga.
5. do some type of breathing exercises 10-20 minutes a day.

Why don't we add:

6. meditate using mindfulness meditation (Chapters 53 and 54).
7. discharge emotion on a regular basis. (I originally tried and I still try to discharge at least once a week. Why should we let stress accumulate?)

CHAPTER 11

ANECDOTE (Not Necessary Information)

<u>For multiple reasons, this afternoon I decided not to let even mild stress accumulate.</u> Why? Because I am a *smart cookie* (an expression from the 1940's—I was born in 1944 so I heard it often). It means I am wise, am *sagacious* (another a cool word).

Anecdote

After doing an errand today I bought coffee and sat in my car, feeling <u>a little</u> stressed out. My stress-producing thought: *all these mostly enjoyable distractions in my life but* **I MUST finish this book!!!**

I did <u>not</u> feel like discharging emotion at all but I knew that feelings of post-discharge relief were real and dependable. I wanted those feelings.

Caffeine is for me a reliable catalyst for tears, has been for decades. Nevertheless, I am skeptical that one small <u>sip</u> of hot coffee could have produced my success, but maybe it did; I retrieved a thought related to my relationships with family members, one that had already proven to be painful, said it aloud, and immediately burst into hot and somewhat bitter tears. Several times I deliberately said the thought aloud and each time briefly (like twenty seconds) cried hard. Then I thought, "I feel better," and thanking aloud those family members that I had brought to mind I drove off, guzzling my strong coffee.

Because I had busted stress I was so unworried about being distracted from writing that I wrote a political Tweet or two (like ten), answered a phone call, searched outdoors for an adored outdoor cat, Twinkletoes, and then, when back in my bedroom, adored my indoor comrade cat, Lilly. Finally...I began writing. I was fifteen minutes behind my writing schedule, which usually frustrates me no end and can cause me to delay writing until the next hour, but there was no frustration. I felt content.

Because I know what works for me I practice skillful emotionality even when it might not seem necessary to do so. As a result I bust stress. I hope the time will come when you take even a hint of stress seriously, and will do the same.

.

CHAPTER 12

THE EMOTIONAL DISCHARGE
<u>EXPERIENCE</u>

Let me repeat myself: if this is your own book, checkmark the familiar and perhaps cross out that which you strongly doubt. Or, checkmark what you agree with and x-out that with which you disagree.

Jump over repetition if you find it irritating.

☐ During *emotional discharge* emotion literally flows through our bodies and into our awareness. We notice subtle and not-so-subtle physical sensations and may perspire or shake. We don't need words to label the various emotions that we experience; we know them without words. More likely than not, during discharge thoughts/ideas, images, and memories, etc., will spontaneously arise. When we notice them they *tell* us, or disclose directly or indirectly, why we feel as we do. We may laugh, then cry, then laugh because laughter releases tension and/or because we detect an irony related either to the emotion we are experiencing or to a situation. The outcome of discharge? Stress is busted. Generally, we feel better: relieved, more relaxed or totally relaxed, less worried, more hopeful even optimistic, happier or downright happy, even exhilarated and joyful, and often (for me, always) grateful for the opportunity to experience emotions and be really, really, really real. (This means a lot to me, obviously.) AND, actually, even more important to me, we feel more ourselves, our genuine selves, and we feel strengthened and empowered. We don't feel like empty shells or as a dear friend said, like ghosts that have no substance and cannot be seen or heard, which is how children/young people can feel when those adults around them fail to provide undistracted, warm or loving, patient, and prolonged attention. They can wonder, "Maybe I'm not worth it; maybe they never wanted me; maybe they don't love me; maybe they don't even remember I'm here."

☐ No matter the significance of a specific thought, idea, memory, image, or subject/issue that activates discharge, we will bust stress. When we discharge emotion while contemplating something deeply painful, (1) the relief we feel is so profound that it boggles the mind, (2) the information that is *unlocked* or automatically retrieved can be very helpful, and (3) we can have a very welcome surge of energy and of enthusiasm for our lives.

☐ Because crying *drains* the emotion(s) out of any specific emotion-activating thought, in a sense stripping the thought bare (clean), any desire, urge, or compulsion that accompanies the thought is also stripped away; then there is no emotion to sustain it. So when a thought includes a compulsion to do something, emotional discharge extinguishes the emotions that would drive us to act on the compulsion. After discharge we may think the thought again and again but nothing happens, emotionally. HOWEVER, when stress builds, the thought can arise and reactivate the emotion/compulsion. <u>So, regularly busting stress is essential.</u>

☐ When we practice skillful emotionality we intentionally bring to mind and pay attention to our painful thoughts so that we can activate and discharge the emotions associated with (or *attached to*) them. Frequently, we recall the incident(s) that generated the emotions; we actually relive it (them); we cry HARD (anger/rage, grief) and the emotional pain then permanently vanishes along with any related desires, urges, and compulsions.

☐ Because of our beliefs and attitudes, most of us won't find crying easy, not at all. Expect that. If we automatically begin thinking negative thoughts about the process of emotional discharge, or about ourselves for thinking of using it, or for using it, we blunt or cancel the

49

desirable effects because those negative thoughts will trigger stress. It is, therefore, essential that we change our attitudes toward this natural physiological process and do this as quickly as possible.

☐ Because of fears and expectations that we acquired as a result of our past experiences with our parents and others, most of us won't find crying in the presence of anyone easy. First, there is the expectation of punishment; far too many of us were punished <u>because</u> we cried. But other fears and expectations often emerge when we least need them. Some of us are so afraid that we will *scare* other people that we can't cry in anyone's company, and we likely will avoid showing our feelings to those closest to us. Some of us may assume that our emotions will disturb others so much that their lives become endangered or, at the least, that they themselves become at risk of *falling apart* at some point solely because of us. (I believe this fear can be a result of childhood misinterpretation of parental reactions. Extremely emotional parents can appear to be out of control to a child.) We may assume that everyone we know will begin to fear our *falling apart*. Yes, all kinds of thoughts and specific fears (I can't list them all) can arise at a time when we only need to <u>do</u> one thing, one natural thing...and you know what I refer to.

☐ The idea of deliberately allowing ourselves to be emotional to the point of actually crying is quite foreign to most of us. You should know, therefore, that it does not take enormous surges of intense, agonizing emotion to elicit the tears required for the process to be effective. Once we learn to experience even the most subtle feelings/emotions, trickling tears for seconds are an adequate start and should produce a beneficial effect as long as our follow-up thoughts aren't negative.

☐ You should know, also, that if we have not cried for a long time or if we have no recollection of ever having cried (common belief), we will tend to immediately stop crying the moment we hear our own voices. Stress-busting is instantly terminated. There is a simple solution: play highly stimulating and/or beautiful music so loudly that you cannot hear yourself when you begin emotional discharge.

☐ Many people say this to me, "If I start crying I will never stop." They assume that this is true because they know that for years, even decades, they have been holding in their emotions (is this you?), and I have yet to persuade anyone who believes this that they truly are mistaken. Yes, they can't predict how long they will weep or laugh, but discharge will cease when they have obtained adequate relief   Some of us who think we will never stop, do so in minutes. Tears can trickle or flow off and on for

51

days, also. We need to learn that this is okay. No more time limits on our own or anyone else's emotional discharge.

☐ When practicing *skillful emotionality*, you will take charge of your feelings and emotions in a new and revolutionary way—instead of ignoring, discounting, denying, or burying them, you will become adept at choosing (A) when to experience emotion, (B) with whom to experience emotion if you want company, (C) the level of emotional intensity for which you are prepared, and, (D) the length of time that you want to actually *allow* emotion(to occur). You are in control!

☐ You are going to develop emotion tolerance, not only for your own emotions but for the emotions of others. Their emotionality will not faze you one bit. In fact, you will gladly and patiently let them "have their emotions" so they can de-stress. (You will no longer feel compelled to comfort them with pats or hugs.) De-stressed, everyone thinks more clearly and is able to be more patient, less impulsive and compulsive, even more loving.

☐ You also are going to develop emotional resilience because you will have become, during *practice*, increasingly able to experience the full range of human emotions without discomfort, anxiety, fear, or dread.

Among other things, this means you will not have to avoid situations or people that tend to trigger stress.

☐ You will be ready to face Reality. With emotional resilience we are relatively invulnerable to self-deception and delusion. (Conscious and subconscious fear of our feelings and emotions prevents us from consciously acknowledging accurate, factual information.)

☐ Whether you like it or not, you will begin to feel deeper empathy for everyone you encounter (or read about or see—on TV, on the Internet, etc.). This increase in empathy will enable you to have richer relationships, and life will become even more meaningful and fulfilling than it was before. Because of my experience, I believe that your sensitivity to the needs of humanity and all other forms of life on Earth will increase noticeably. I went from no genuine empathy to universal empathy, all with no regret. Trust me, *Life* is more precious when we are able to deeply *feel* it and *feel* the lives of other precious beings including the human.

☐ It is important to note that certain medical problems as well as certain medications may in some way interfere with the discharge process, reducing or eliminating the beneficial effects or preventing the process from occurring at all. Some medications, especially psychiatric medications, make it difficult or nearly impossible to activate or prolong the emotional discharge process.

Emotional discharge is a life-and-spirit enrichment process.

♥

So what might learning to discharge emotion do for you?

Next chapter, let's see what it did for me.

After you read that next chapter, if you like what you hear, why not return to this page and follow these directions: think this thought five times — *I promise, from now on, to remind myself that discharging emotion is a rational and therapeutic thing for me, and for anyone else, to do. To discharge is normal not abnormal. It is <u>NOT DISCHARGING</u> that is ABNORMAL.*

CHAPTER 13

MY *PRACTICE* BENEFITS #1

Although you probably have been conditioned to think negatively about emotional discharge—after all, who have you seen cry lately who didn't react with embarrassment, humiliation, or shame plus apologies once they stopped crying—you may not have been conditioned to automatically think negatively about others' <u>positive</u> experiences with it, like mine.

Here are all my benefits from practice.

1. I learned to prevent depression/mood swings by keeping my stress level low.
2. I learned to recognize the thoughts and ideas, interests, longings and desires, and behaviors that were likely to arise when I was avoiding painful feelings/emotions.
3. Recognition enabled me to activate the discharge process and <u>bust stress</u> before I became overwhelmed and in danger of becoming depressed or harmfully high/intense.
4. I learned to intentionally activate the discharge process at the time of my own choosing and as a result I was able to thoroughly experience and therefore reduce the intensity of, or terminate completely, these distressing/painful emotions, whenever they arose: nervousness, apprehension,

worry, fear (felt it once), irritation, frustration, anger, rage, sadness, grief, anguish, regret, remorse, bitterness, loneliness, and ambivalence (not sure is an emotion).

You might ask me, "Well, wouldn't it have been more sensible to ignore or bury those painful feelings and emotions?   They cause stress."

My answer is, "They <u>cause</u> stress only because we hold them tightly in.   If we discharge them we then feel relief and can more easily think about what has evoked those feelings/emotions."

CHAPTER 14

MY *PRACTICE* BENEFITS #2

If you are still thinking about putting this book down for any reason, please don't. The rewards of allowing this natural process are so SO far from trivial. If my life were to be summarized on a timeline, this is what it would look like—

No depression & no highs. (I had lost the capacity to experience painful feelings and emotions.)

No depression, harmful mood swings, or obsessions. If I suspect stress or a tendency to get depressed or high, I practice *skillful emotionality.*

Depression & highs experienced as "intensity periods. " A few obsessions.

Check out the next page to see what else my life would look like on a timeline.

Little awareness of self and others, no insight, no genuine empathy, and no tolerance for emotional suffering. Absolutely no emotional resilience. Pleasure and excitement only.

Awareness of self and others, normal level of insight, nearly universal empathy, and high tolerance for the full range of human emotions from anguish and bitterness to joy. Emotional resilience achieved.

Growing awareness of self and others, some insight, limited empathy, developing ability to notice stress and experience some emotional pain.

Yes, I had very serious *invisible* problems when I was growing up and they remained unchanged until I fell apart completely and was forced to *reassemble* myself. (I hope that you didn't fall apart completely but perhaps you did; if so, I am so sorry, but I have confidence that you, like me, can reassemble yourself while taking charge of your life. Do not give up!!!)

I want you to understand this: I strongly believe that most of my problems may never have developed had I been able to discharge emotion with my parents and as a result regularly bust stress and remain bonded with them. (I suspect that the same could be said about all of us.) Not that firm bonding and stress-busting are the only benefits of discharge. Far from it!! By the time you read the last page of this book you will know precisely what I mean.

So in the end, what did I get out of learning to practice emotional discharge? Only a life that didn't end too soon because of a suicidal depression, only a life that didn't take anyone else's life, only a life that didn't become a scary seesaw of unmanageable and occasionally harmful or dangerous highs, and only a life that included meaningful relationships and, eventually (like most recently), a regained ability to be truly present with others and love and care about them with awareness and at least some wisdom.

Yup, our brains and the process are...

AWESOME!

CHAPTER 15

OUR BRAINS ARE EMOTIONAL AND THEY ARE TALKING TO US—WE MUST LISTEN TO AND TRUST THEM

This is the slogan that we need to adopt—

TRUST THE BRAIN

According to the most recent research (March, 2017), the brain, our amazingly complex organ that possesses approximately eighty-six billion interconnected neurons (not 100 billion) that talk both with one another and with our entire body, knows exactly what we need to do in order to reduce or eliminate feelings of stress and distress. It tells us what to do—with spoken messages (our thoughts) and with physical sensation!   If we want to regularly bust stress we must learn to pay attention to it and take its messages seriously even though we can't always immediately act on them.

If you suddenly think, "I'm angry," or "I need to cry," you have received a spoken *message* in the form of a sudden (often faint, though) thought (consider it an observation).

IF you use the thought to activate discharge, the anger and the need to cry will diminish or vanish once the tears stop.

If you suddenly notice:

- a strange tickling sensation inside your lower eyelids,
- a sensation of tears *behind* your eyes,
- the welling of tears in your eyes,
- tightening of the muscles of your forehead or any faint sensation in the forehead area,
- scalp chills and tingles which may chase up one side of your head or the other, flow over your head from any direction, or instantly encompass your entire skull,
- sudden sharp pain in your forehead, temple, or back of your head,
- tightness in throat, sudden change in your voice or problem with talking clearly,
- clenching of teeth and fists,
- a really subtle sensation in the center of your torso or near the heart area, or
- sudden muscle tension anywhere in your body, then—

you have received a message in the form of sensations and you would benefit from promptly discharging emotion and busting stress.

When I realize that I need to discharge emotion but can't (because of circumstances) I often write down what I was thinking before the sensations occurred. I also list the feelings, distinct thoughts, and memories/images, you name it, that have emerged and are emerging. With practice we do become extremely skillful at noticing what our excellent brains are doing.

Suppose you are driving along in your car or walking or riding a bike, feeling great (or not), and suddenly you feel your eyes fill with tears. You could not possibly receive a more direct message than that, could you? Loud and clear, your brain is telling you, "Discharge emotion! Activate the process now! I need it. I will benefit from it. Believe me!"

Your brain really is a precision instrument.

We all, worldwide, have learned to ignore, discount, deny, and bury/cancel/delete these verbal *messages* and these sensation. The price of doing so can be and often is, exorbitant. Stress builds because we don't realize that we are having coping problems. We don't seek solutions. We don't ask for help. We crash psychologically. Sometimes we harm ourselves and/or others. If we are in decision-making positions we can do great and irreversible harm.

For most of our lives our social programming has convincingly told us *there's no need for crying.* Therefore, it is extremely hard (or impossible) for us to believe that <u>the brain sends ONLY necessary messages when it concerns our need to bust stress and discharge emotion</u>. **Only necessary messages!**

Our brains truly are brilliant protectors of our health. They evolved to serve us effectively and efficiently which means they evolved to help us bust stress and think clearly—at every moment, and...

emotional discharge is the app for that.

So, in spite of what we have been taught to believe about crying/laughing with tears (emotional discharge), we <u>must</u> take the physical sensations, the thought messages, and the usually messy emotional discharge process seriously. We <u>must</u> reject the socially conditioned beliefs about, and attitudes toward, crying and tears which have prevented us from utilizing the process.

Gradually, by <u>freeing ourselves from the crippling burden of negative attitudes and false beliefs</u> about the process, we reduce the likelihood that depression and harmful mood swings will again dominate our lives. (If you don't have a vulnerability to stress-induced depression/mood swings, you, too, will benefit from the process, believe me.)

Remember, learning how to quickly reduce and even eliminate stress has enormous value both short term and long term, for all of us. As science is proving, stress, especially unabated and chronic stress, takes a heavy toll:

- physically,
- mentally/intellectually,
- emotionally, and
- spiritually.

This process that I cherish so highly because it has enriched my life is not an accessory, is not something that makes something else more useful. It *is* us, is an integral part of us. <u>REPEAT: it is *not* an accessory. It **is** us.</u>

TEARS
AND EMOTION
R

US!

CHAPTER 16

EMOTIONS REALLY R US

Visualize this: you are examining your face in a bathroom mirror; your cheeks already are gleaming and slippery with tears. Suddenly, your lips twist downward, your mouth opens, you begin to sob so hard that you gasp, and you grab the edge of the sink so that you don't lose your balance. For a few moments you can hardly catch your breath and mucous streams from your nose like water (you expertly catch all of it with handfuls of toilet paper).

And then it is over. You stop crying. You mop up. Someone from the next room calls out, "You did it! You finally did it!"

You walk into that room, still mopping your face, and flop on the couch next to your companion. You say, "Thanks for listening to me. I couldn't let you see my face. It looks so ugly. But knowing you could hear me helped a lot. I'm still not ready to talk about anything, but what happened when I was a kid really hurt."

Tears begin to leak from your eyes but now you decide to set your emotions aside and say to your companion, "I really thank you. I do feel better. Can I listen to you? Anything you want to say or feel? You deserve real attention, too."

What has happened? I think it is obvious. Despite the social programming that persuaded you crying makes you look ugly, you nevertheless accepted and made use of your emotional nature. Although you weren't ready to talk about what happened to you at some point in your life, your tears busted stress so that you felt better and therefore thought to give caring attention to your companion. You became, in fact, a model for your friend who, despite the enthusiastic response to your crying, no doubt was as programmed as you to avoid the discharge process.

Yes, our brains are precision instruments and they generate an awesome number of distinct feelings and emotions. Evolution, or Creation (you choose), has ensured this. We are born with this capacity, but why? Does our species actually needs this capability...or is it overkill?

Overkill, not at all! Because every setting and situation that we encounter has unique elements and because the human social world is truly complex, our bodies/brains must have the capacity to detect the most subtle indications of stress and potential harm. Thoughts, feelings, and emotions are our messengers. We must have the capacity to feel/experience a *shockingly broad range of distinct feelings/emotions* so that we are able to intelligently and healthfully navigate the real human social world with intelligence, wisdom, empathy, and compassion.

Our brains are so finely tuned to have meaningful and rewarding human social interactions and experiences that if we want to actually have them we are simply going to have to accept the fact that emotions really are us and it is our inherited process of emotional discharge that makes everything work—and work well. In fact, and I may have forgotten to tell you this, psychological and MRI research has provided good evidence that all of our decisions, one way or another, are based on emotion whether or not we are aware of emotion. The individual who claims, "I base all my decisions on logic, not on emotion," simply is WRONG.

Is it *good* that emotion underlies all human decision-making? It has to be; it is emotion, not intellect, that makes us human and humane. Without emotion we are robots. Robots.

Now, final say: if you have access to a computer and the Internet, you will find a rather comprehensive list of human feelings and emotions at this website, if the website still exists:

http://psychologia.co/list-of-human-emotions/

REMEMBER WHAT YOU READ ON THE VERY NEXT PAGE...

EMOTIONS

R

US!

And it truly is okay!!   In fact, it is meant to be!

CHAPTER 17

OUR BRAINS *DO THEIR BEST* BUT WE DO HAVE A SIGNIFICANT HANDICAP AND WE MUST REMEMBER WHAT IT IS BECAUSE THEN WE WON'T BE SO HARD ON OURSELVES

(Very Short Title Don't You Think)

Our excellent brains use our past experiences to create responses to presently occurring experiences.   Because of this we are likely, in any given situation, especially when we are under stress and therefore unable to notice the unique elements of situations, to automatically respond in the present as we did in the past even though no two situations are ever truly identical.   When that happens, the process involved is called, by many of us who learned to discharge emotion, *restimulation*.   You will find two examples of my own experiences with it in Chapter 19.

Our significant handicap is a simple one: we often are unable to recognize *restimulation* when it takes place. The good news is, we can learn to eliminate this handicap or at least prevent it from ruling our lives.   You will see what I mean.

Here is a familiar example of *restimulation*.   We meet a stranger and almost instantly we like, bond with, even love, them.   Do we ask ourselves, "Why do I feel this way?" Are we determined to uncover an explanation for our immediate reaction to this person? Do we interrogate ourselves? My guess is, *no*. Most of us don't. (I didn't interrogate myself when that happened to me. I am glad that I didn't, too.)

Yes, a stranger appears and reminds us, either consciously or unconsciously, of someone we already feel close to, have bonded with, and/or love. Something about them: physical characteristic(s), personality trait(s), mannerism(s), way of moving their bodies or gesturing, tone of voice, choice of words and inflection, content of their conversation, hairstyle, piece of jewelry (men's or women's) preference for clothing or food, attitudes, beliefs, values, even the situation and circumstances of our encounter—endless list, you see—reminds us of that other person so that we automatically respond to this stranger in the same way, or nearly the same way, that we had responded to, or are still responding to, the person that we already know, and *that* is *restimulation*.

When stress is present and at least one element in a current environment/situation is sufficiently similar to one in the past, then specific thoughts, memories, feelings, emotions, and/or behaviors from the past <u>can</u> be reactivated, re-stimulated (restimulated). Actually, it happens all the time; it certainly did in my life as a response to stress. In present time, simply because of unrecognized stress, I was likely to:

1. feel the same feelings and/or
2. experience the same emotions, and/or
3. think the same thoughts, and/or
4. make the same assumptions, and/or
5. draw the same conclusion, and/or;
6. accept without question the same beliefs and attitudes, and/or
7. make the same decisions, and/or
8. want to take the same courses of action

that I did in the past.

Does the similarity, past to present, have to be glaring? Indeed not. Please remember this: it can be shockingly obscure. Here is an example of *shockingly obscure*—a stranger that we are scheduled to meet is standing on the sidewalk in front of a store window clock display. Although our attention is focused on this individual, we semi-awarely spy in our periphery a replica of an antique clock that resembles the wall clock in our long-deceased and adored grandmother or grandfather's living room where we always had cookies and milk and played computer games. The clock is activating feelings of happiness and camaraderie while we are talking with this stranger and we feel an inexplicable rapport and closeness that we never think to question.

Might our response to this person present us with a problem? Sure! We might automatically be convinced, *this encounter is meant to be and she/he is my soul mate.*

(That could be true, of course. Only time will tell.) Or, possibly we will decide to invest our life savings in this obviously trustworthy stranger—who never will invest it at all.

Why should those of us who are vulnerable to depression/mood swings know about the process of *restimulation*? Because we can be really hard on ourselves when *things go wrong* and we need to know that forgiveness-of-self really is justified. Whether we are swinging up or down or up and down, feelings of helplessness, hopelessness, and even self-hatred can occur when things *go wrong* (words italicized because we may only think that they have gone wrong), and we must, at those times, remind ourselves that in some way *restimulation probably is involved.* There always is a logical reason for each decision and action. Many are at least partially the result of restimulation. Some people would argue that all non-constructive and/or harmful responses to external events are the result of restimulation. Not true, of course. Restimulation can save our lives. Two of the personal anecdotes that I provide in Chapter 19 are good examples of the potential of restimultion.

Remember, because we are vulnerable to depression/mood swings and to being ever so hard on ourselves, it is helpful to keep in mind:

I am a good person. I am intelligent.

I am strong.   I am brave.
I am NOT a failure.   I am NOT undesirable.   I am
NOT worthless or delicate or weak!!
NO!   NO!   NO!
I probably reacted in the present the same way that
I reacted in the past, but I am learning to recognize
restimulation when it is occurring.
Reducing stress on a regular basis will always help.

Each of us has a powerful brain.   You, me, everyone.
Our stupendously complex brains evolved or were created
to respond rationally, constructively, and creatively to
absolutely everything that happens, but in order to allow
them do this we need to do two things:

1. keep stress low.
2. experience our emotions while noticing thoughts,
   feelings, memories, etc.

**So, love your brain!   It is not your enemy.
It is one of your best friends.
Contrary to what you may think, it is eager
to serve you well, but you need to help it
do that.   Like me, let it discharge emotion
when it needs to.**

CHAPTER 18

RESTIMULATION MADE ME DO IT SO *AM I INNOCENT?*

Guess what!   You really <u>are</u> innocent!

If restimulation plays such a major role in our lives, and it can affect us without our knowing it, why is it fair to hold us responsible for our actions?   Can we always claim innocence?   If so, might the practices and viewpoints of skillful emotionality encourage irresponsibility?

Good questions!   I must say this right now so that some of you don't immediately throw this book in the trash, **"We all <u>are</u> innocent but we are still responsible for our actions."**   Next, read the best news!

We humans naturally feel responsible and want to be held responsible!

"Sure, yeah, and where's the proof?"

I am going to attempt to provide you with some proof.

Why has the issue of responsibility come up? Because someone that I know responded to my definition of restimulation with something akin to horror. They then angrily accused me of rhapsodizing about a practice that teaches irresponsibility. (I have, in fact, spoken with several individuals who reacted similarly when I tried to explain restimulation to them. My explanations are obviously nothing to be proud of. I hope that the following explanation *works*.)

There really is no conflict when it comes to restimulation, innocence, and responsibility. While we discharge emotion (1) we usually uncover evidence that our past poor judgment and non-constructive or possibly harmful behavior indeed was to some degree the result of restimulation, and, (2) we usually discover that accepting responsibility actually feels good. It is, in fact, natural (instinctive) for us to feel responsible for our thoughts and actions and the brain, our esteemed organ of precision, actually needs us to take responsibility for our actions.

> Here is a suggestion for you! Skip the next sections of this chapter if the issues of restimulation, innocence, and responsibility bore you. Otherwise...

The truth about responsibility is at the least three-fold. You may strenuously disagree with every statement! If you do, I really <u>do</u> understand. In my past these arguments may have meant little even to me!

The Truth About Responsibility
Statement #1

The human brain causes us, at birth, to naturally <u>feel</u> responsible for our own actions since we most definitely are responsible...for our own survival. <u>This sense of responsibility is instinctive and serves us well as we mature.</u> Without it our species would be nonexistent. (It is not the fault of our infant selves that we actually have little ability to protect and feed ourselves.)

I am not basing this assertion on textbook knowledge alone. I, like many practitioners of emotional discharge, have inadvertently (no intention to do so) relived my birth as well as specific moments in infancy. During one infancy experience I *knew* that I <u>had</u> to actively look for eye-shapes even though I did not know that eye shapes meant human beings, safety, and food. During another reliving, with my arms upraised, I anxiously watched strips of color that were stacked on top of each other. I desperately wanted the strips to grow larger and when they failed to do so I felt fear.

If you guessed correctly that expanding strips of color meant whatever I was intently watching had moved closer to me, you are right; I *knew* color strips would grow larger if what I wanted to happen was going to happen. I did not know I was watching humans and their colorful clothing. Most definitely, I felt responsible for securing the response I needed and in this instance I was not successful. The color strips, my parents, walked past me.

The Truth About Responsibility
Statement #2

We evolved, or were created, as beings who naturally seek pleasurable social interactions as well as warm, loving, and supportive relationships. Our ***instinctive*** ability to instantly experience grief, guilt, regret, and remorse when others suffer because of our actions produces a longing to repair relationships. If we have not been programmed to ignore, discount, deny, and bury painful emotions we automatically seek the warm, focused, and prolonged attention either of the individual(s) we have hurt or of others with whom we are comfortable. We do this so that we can discharge and bond again with those we have hurt.

The Truth About Responsibility
Statement #3

Believe me, evolution/Creation, has made sure that we humans feel good when we accept full responsibility for our actions. Among other feelings and emotions that we experience when we accept responsibility, are: (1) profound relief when we admit that our actions have hurt others, and (2) gratitude when others who are important to us acknowledge what we have done and forgive us <u>as</u> we forgive ourselves.

The End, Almost

Do most of us seem to want to accept responsibility for our actions?   It might not seem that we do, but I tell you, when we receive warm support from others for <u>all</u> of our painful emotions, the desire to be responsible and to be held accountable increases, perhaps slowly but at least inexorably.   That is the experience of those who regularly practice emotional discharge.   That has been my experience.

If you presently have regrets or feel remorse, I hope that will be your experience, also.   I think that it will be.   Be patient with yourself...and also with others.

CHAPTER 19

ANECDOTES—TWO EXPERIENCES WITH *RESTIMULATION*

<u>(Not Necessary Information)</u>

Correction: This paragraph <u>is</u> necessary.

Restimulation plays a major role in our lives. Not only can it cause us to react to people and to situations in ways that might be less rewarding and constructive or harmful or more harmful than they otherwise would be, it can cause us to find certain activities more <u>difficult,</u> <u>intimidating,</u> <u>scary,</u> <u>or frightening</u> than they otherwise would be.

EXAMPLE #1

I am trying to add a column of expenses without the benefit of a calculator or computer. It is a short column! Nevertheless, I become so tense that I can't concentrate and I quit. My tension makes no sense and I am unbelievably frustrated. I decide to activate discharge and think about how I am feeling. A thought arises out of nowhere. It triggers grief and I begin to cry. Suddenly, I see in my mind's eye the kitchen table and a grayish sheet of arithmetic paper. I realize that I am quite small, sitting at the kitchen table with my mom, trying to complete a simple addition problem. I keep making mistakes and am extremely upset with myself because addition doesn't yet make sense to me.   I was a premie, born by Cesarean at least seven weeks early, and when I began kindergarten and later first grade I was not ready for any abstract concepts whatsoever...like the concepts of time and clocks and of numbers and calculation   When my teachers and my mom tried to help me I always felt anxiety, always felt *dumb*, always dreaded their assistance.

EXAMPLE #2

I consider this to be a major example.   It illustrates how in the present, <u>stress alone</u> can activate thoughts/ideas, feelings, emotions, and desires that earlier in our lives had emerged when we were experiencing unrelieved stress.

In 1968, stress and the stress-activated restimulation of a set of violence-related fantasies that had distracted and entertained me as a child, required that first hospital.   In 1971, more than a full year after my discharge from Vermont State Hospital, due to unrecognized stress I nearly succumbed to restimulation of the very same violence-related fantasies.

I was still living in beautiful Burlington, Vermont, working in the general hospital as a tray girl.   My relationship with two older male friends was beginning to trigger stress, stress to which I responded with a mood swing up, way up, whenever I was in their company.

One day, as I ambled past a store display that included silver figurines of jousting knights wielding beautiful lances, I felt a stirring of interest and thought, "Buy it. Buy two." I had the feeling that ownership, that holding the figurines and also looking at them on a bookshelf, would make me feel *good*.

So, I was about to enter the store with cash in hand when a wave of anxiety hit...and I fled. What had happened? Restimulation! I didn't realize it but the knights' lances had reminded me of weaponry and instantly evoked a vague feeling that I might start thinking scary thoughts if I purchased them. I had no suspicion as to what the scary thoughts were because I didn't have the emotional tolerance to become conscious of what they were, but I knew one thing: purchasing them was going to be a very VERY bad idea.

Fortunately, I didn't buy them. Their constant *companionship* definitely would have restimulated unconscious thoughts and feelings whenever I looked at or held them. Their presence may have pushed me past the breaking point at which time every unwanted thought might have erupted.

All of our brains possess the awesome ability to calculate, based on association, all possible trajectories for our every thought and action. (All hail the marvelous brain!)

If you like equations, here is one:

Stress + at least one feature or element that is <u>common to</u> at least one past experience and to the current environment/situation = restimulation

Or, if E equals common element, Stress + E = Restimulation

Stress + the knights' lances = the sense that unwanted thoughts would be restimulated/reactivated.

CHAPTER 20

LET'S <u>REALLY</u> FEEL SORRY FOR OURSELVES AND HAVE A *PITY PARTY*

Have you ever heard that expression, *pity party*? Just wondered. I hadn't, until recently. Guess that I am truly lucky.

A good friend of mine who is under a great deal of stress states that she will not cry (1) because she doesn't feel sorry for herself, (2) when people cry they are feeling sorry for themselves, and (3) she doesn't believe that it is healthy for us to feel sorry for ourselves. Can't you just hear the voices of frustrated adults admonishing their weeping children with, "Stop feeling sorry for yourself. It's not good for you."

Was that ever said to you? If it was, I am sorry. Forgive the speaker(s). They, like you, were victims of social programming.

Another good friend believes that when two people get together to practice skillful emotionality (emotional discharge) they are convening nothing more than an ill-advised, harmful *pity party*—his words. Pity parties...are they harmful or are they useful? Good grief, we need answers!

I thank both friends for bringing to my attention this extremely common viewpoint. It is likely that they both were taught early-and-often, while growing up, to believe that crying is a pity party, a harmful and shameful exercise in feeling sorry for ourselves. (Remember, big boys don't cry and big girls don't, either! For more on this, see Chapter 58 right now).

Naturally, because of their programming neither of my friends sees any value in their crying or for that matter in anyone else's crying. (Both, however, will allow spontaneous tears in others and even provide silent, uncritical attention.) Their inability to cry greatly saddens me since each of them has survived some major disappointments as well as losses and deserves the opportunity to bust stress and heal wounds.

So here is a question for you: has anyone ever said to you when you began to cry, "Stop feeling sorry for yourself." For a moment, please think about that. Can you estimate the number of times you heard those words, if you did? It matters—the more frequently you heard them the more frequently you probably felt embarrassment or shame, felt bad about who you were, and perhaps even hated yourself and wanted to be someone else (or dead), all because you consciously or unconsciously wanted and needed to cry but literally were made to feel terrible about yourself because of this.

If you heard those words a lot it most likely will take a determined effort to repair your attitude toward discharge and also retrain your brain so that it is capable of activating the discharge process the moment you wish to do so, but you <u>can</u> do it!   I promise!   You will succeed! The skills we all use in this practice will help you activate the process.

With each breakthrough to tears you will need to celebrate your liberation with— *I did it!   I did it!   Yay for me!*

Yes, I think that a lot of us (though not me) heard those words when we were young.   Interestingly enough, although I don't recall ever hearing those words said to me there surely was someone in my family who did hear them—my grandmother.   According to my mom, one day when I was in my playpen and my mom and her mom were sitting in the living room with me, I began to cry. My grandmother said to my mom, "I think she wants you to pick her up." My mom's response? "No, she's just feeling sorry for herself."

My mom had learned that viewpoint, of course, and perhaps I did hear those words after all. I will never know. However, I know this: this common viewpoint, that we are doing nothing more than feeling sorry for ourselves when we discharge emotion, is one that we learn from parents and then inject, like an anesthetic (numbing agent) into the minds of our own children.

You notice that I label those words *numbing agents*? I do so because that is what they are. Whatever our age, those words shut us down and numb us out when they are spoken to us. Real life-changing life-ending damage can be the result. In the next chapter I explain what I mean.

CHAPTER 21

IT AIN'T NO PITY PARTY IF IT SAVES MY LIFE **<u>AND</u>** YOURS

If someone you know considers crying a *pity party* there probably is little you can do to enlighten them, at least immediately. If someone you know happens to see tears in your eyes and with a smirk or a snarl responds with, "Pity party! Stop feeling sorry for yourself," there probably <u>is</u> something that you can do: without being confrontational say, "Crying busts stress, so as far as pity parties go I'm going to have all the pity parties I need so I feel good, and I am going to have one right now. If you like, after mine you have one, too."

If because of your kind offer they tear up, say, "Go for it!"
<u>And boy, will you bust stress</u>

Now that is the somewhat light treatment of a terribly serious subject. Next, the heavy treatment of a terribly serious subject. Get ready!

I don't know how many of us were accused of holding solo or group *pity parties*, but I am sure a good number of us were told, "Stop feeling sorry for yourself." Definitely, those words were a prescription for depression/mood swings, possible self-isolation, maybe self-loathing, and perhaps even worse. How so? Over time, if we heard such words frequently enough while we were growing up, we became at risk of associating <u>all painful feelings that arise</u>, and would discharge in tears, with feeling sorry for ourselves: *If I feel unhappy and sad I am feeling sorry for myself. If I cry I will <u>really</u> be feeling sorry for myself. Everyone will think that I am feeling sorry for myself. That's called self-pity and self-pity is selfish and weak. I must make sure absolutely no one ever knows how I feel.*

Ideas like that, especially for those of us who are male (not me, of course), can become fatal. Think about it.

Suppose you are a guy (unless you are not)...as the years pass, stress never gets busted. Year after year each separate and distinct painful emotion activated by circumstance deposits in your good heart and mind *layers* (figuratively speaking) of painful emotion felt and unfelt. Your health suffers.

Psychologically, you are in solitary emotional-confinement. You are never free to be yourself, to show yourself, to be real with those you care about and love. You feel unbearably alone. You have so much painful emotion to conceal that if you aren't yet emotionally numb you have moments of fear or rage. No one has rescued you.

Will you ever get to be real, to show your emotions, to cry off emotional pain? We all can hope that you will, but perhaps you won't

So what might ultimately happen beside depression/mood swings? Suicide? Homicide with a specific target or targets? A massive *explosion* in violence affecting large numbers of strangers...and then suicide?

Whether you are male or female, hear this: your life is precious. On the next page you will find a statement you deserve to hear.

If you feel overwhelmed by life, I beg you, do not explode unless it is with emotion.

Your life, yes, your <u>own</u> life, is far too precious to lose though unwise or harmful or acts of any kind.   All you really need to do is to regularly let out a ton of feelings/emotions using nice wet messy tears with sobbing.   Yes, it will take time.

Right now, tell someone how you are feeling; yes, risk their response.   Don't let embarrassment or shame stop you,
PLEASE.

Or head for an emergency room and let them know that you feel like exploding.

Or keep reading this book or find a copy of **THE PRIMAL SCREAM**.   (See Chapter 50 in this book.)

You are an innocent victim of social programming and you CAN eliminate that programming and stay alive, not only stay alive but reassemble yourself as I did and discover that you, like me, are capable of achieving happiness and fulfillment.

Emotional discharge…is it a *pity party* or a *life saver*?   No debate!   Make it your own personal LIVE SAVER.   TODAY!

I want you to

save your life!

Yes, I do.

CHAPTER 22

IS IT <u>REALLY</u> OKAY IF I FEEL SORRY FOR MYSELF?

Is it?   Of course it is.   Such feelings arise only for logical reasons and when they are suppressed they add to stress. Since you want to bust stress you are going to discharge emotion; you are going to cry your eyes out and your heart and health back in!

Can crying <u>for</u> ourselves be harmful?   This fear certainly exists if we have been conditioned by our early childhood experiences to believe that it is harmful: *Honey, you will never make it in this world by being a cry-baby.* However, because fear causes stress the most rapid-acting antidote to fear <u>is</u> discharge.

I had a friend who was dying.   Cancer.   She cried once that I know of.   I had hoped that I could help her bust stress and shed some grief, so I asked her who, dead or alive, she really wished she could talk to (one of the *skills* we learn to use, as needed).   She quickly replied, "My dad."   I next asked her what she needed to say to him.   I don't recall what she said, but briefly she wept hard.

From her comments afterwards I realized that no one that she knew was comfortable with tears or recognized their value.   Therefore, no one was able to provide her with the patient, loving attention that she deserved for grieving her upcoming loss of life. (Truthfully, this is a tragic situation for far too many us.) As she was in hospice, I encouraged her to ask for a hospice counselor. No. Her lifetime of emotional suppression had erected a barrier that she was able to penetrate, but only once.

Considering the benefits of discharge, including what I believe to be reduction in inflammation and strengthening of the immune system, her death may have been easier. I will never know if it could have been. If I become ill with cancer I will use this process regularly. Perhaps my tears will (leak) eke out some clues.

Won't you join me in enlightening those who erroneously believe that crying, that emotional discharge, is nothing more than indulging ourselves and feeling sorry for ourselves, and that when we cry with others, perhaps even in small groups, we are convening rather disgusting pity parties. We need to help them understand that it is wise to cry for ourselves because tears bust stress.

Tears bust stress! In fact, to the brain, tears are like oxygen: essential!

CHAPTER 23

ANECDOTES—MY TWO RECENT *PITY PARTIES*

And now, personal tales that are <u>not necessary reading</u>.

I don't just talk pity parties, I do them, even when I am alone with me-myself-and-I! Twice recently I busted stress when I successfully cried for myself. I was alone, driving, both times when the impulse arose.

For the first *party*, I was driving. Feeling overwhelmed and sorry for myself, I emphatically said, "I am REALLY feeling sorry for myself." Because I am an expert discharger I instantly burst into heavy tears. For about thirty seconds I cried so hard and so loudly that I blew the car windows out and floated the car down the street. (What a spectacle.)

For the second *party*, I was feeling sorry for myself because I realized that an ill chicken that I had come to love (true!) and care for had died unnecessarily. Chix, the Rhode Island Red chicken who loved her food, especially lentils and rice, and who seemed to rejoice in running gracefully for treats, would have lived longer had I been well informed about chicken health. She paid the price for my ignorance and I still am heartbroken.

Yes, I <u>was</u> responsible for her death so I felt sorry for myself. I cried. I felt better. She was dead and I felt better.

You may think, "Pam's not *responsible* for the death. It just happened. And it was just a chicken, anyway!" If that is your present reaction to my story I do understand. However, for the rest of my life I refuse, that is I hope that I will refuse, to <u>ignore, discount, deny, and bury</u> any feelings that naturally arise. I have fought too long and hard to experience the full range of emotions to intentionally reactivate a pattern of emotion-avoidance.

Please, remember that it is human to feel sorry for yourself, to grieve for yourself, and it is brilliant and wise to cry the sorrow out as needed. If you want company when you allow yourself to experience these emotions, invite someone to exchange attention with you.

CHAPTER 24

RESILIENCE AND TOUGHNESS—JUST WHAT WE NEED

Nothing could be more important than this reminder: we possess genuine resilience not when nothing upsets us much or at all but when those things that do upset us are reacted to thoughtfully and effectively. And what do I mean by *effectively*?

Effectively means that we have no need to avoid individuals and situations and we never have to run away from ourselves. *Effectively* mean that we are capable of experiencing our emotions. It means that we can discharge emotion and bust stress as needed, without apprehension, anxiety, panic attacks, or fear. *Effectively* also means that we are able to thoughtfully and successfully employ other practices. (I, for example, find added mental and physical peacefulness as well as warm companionship by meditating in a small group, a sangha, that meets at my church once a week.)

When we are young, because of our parents' (loved ones, care givers, etc.) responses to our natural emotionality, i.e., their facial expressions conveying concern, worry, alarm, annoyance, frustration, anger, sadness, nervousness, anxiety, and even fear, many of us grow up thinking that we must *handle our emotions with kid gloves.* If you never heard the *kid gloves* expression, in this context it means that we must treat our emotions as though we, who possess the emotions, are extremely *delicate.* Delicate.

Well, if we don't know how to quickly bust stress when we need to we can begin to feel overwhelmed and it is likely that some of us will then believe that we are delicate. But we are not delicate. **We are deprived. We have been deprived of encouragement to use our natural stress-buster.** Therefore, we are overstressed, not delicate.

Before leaving this chapter, I want to take a look at dictionary definitions for *resilience.* After you read them, I will tell you why it's important to be aware of the definitions, which include:

1. *the ability to recover quickly from difficulties; toughness* (The Oxford Living Dictionaries) on the Internet.
2. *an ability to recover from or adjust easily to misfortune or change* (Merriam-Webster).
3. *resilience is the process of adapting well in the face of adversity, trauma, tragedy, threats, or even significant sources of stress such as family and relationship problems, serious health problems, or workplace and financial stressors. It means*

bouncing back from difficult experiences.
(https://www.psychcentral.com)

This is why knowing those definitions are important: the ability to bust stress fast using, <u>among other practices and activities</u>, the discharge process, helps us embody through our actions, every one of those definitions. Every single one.

```
EVERY
SINGLE
ONE!!!!
```

As for *toughness*, cited above in the first definition, this is my opinion: we have achieved genuine toughness once we respond to stress and emotional pain this way—

1. automatically or intentionally (sometimes it takes a decision) feel and experience our emotions whether they feel *good* or not.
2. decisively reach out for help if we need it.

Each of the above responses to Life's demands can be scary, but because we have toughness we take action! I have long thought that I would never again reach out for help because I would be embarrassed, especially after writing this book, but guess what! After typing that last sentence I have changed my mind. I am too tough to deliberately deny myself support and guidance when I need it.   Yeah.

Resilience & toughness are ours when we wield real discharge powers.

The word *wield* reminds me of the Harry Potter series, written by J.K. Rowling, and the expert wielding of magic wands.   To me the most valuable magic wand would be one we could expertly wield with one another so that when any of us were *touched* by a wand's energy we would feel so safe and cared about that we could face, feel, and thoughtfully experience, and gain insight from, the most painful emotions imaginable.

Do you feel resilient right now?   Tough right now?

If you don't <u>feel</u> resilient or tough, remember, you are precious.   With patience and perhaps the help of others, including professionals, you can achieve both resilience and toughness.   You really are worth fighting for!!!

A little repetition—

A GOOD STRESS-BUSTING TOOLKIT CONTAINS LOTS OF *TOOLS* INCLUDING EMOTIONAL DISCHARGE!!

CHAPTER 25

DISCHARGE AND EMOTIONAL PAIN—THE GAIN IS WORTH THE PAIN

I have long been convinced that our only genuine obstacle to successful use of this process is the social programming we received growing up. I have assumed that when we changed our beliefs and attitudes and learned discharge skills we would easily be able to discharge emotion. But I forgot about one thing that, whether we are adults or children, apparently plays a huge role in our decisions to discharge or not discharge. It's called...well...see a conversation that I had with my brother which explains it all. I was interviewing him for this book.

Me: *Do you remember a time when you were young and you wanted to cry or you felt like crying, but you didn't?*

Bruce: *Well, it's not that simple. I remember being confused. It was easy to cry when I got hurt. But it got confusing if things were only going wrong. I didn't know whether to cry or not. Crying hurt. I didn't want to hurt.*

Had I expected him to say that? No. I thought that he'd describe an experience with our mom or dad or with some adult or a peer where his crying had in some way been discouraged.

I am so glad that I asked him that question. Because I have such positive results when I discharge I had totally forgotten that crying <u>does</u> hurt, every time, but only at first. (Those natural opioid painkillers kick in fast if we avoid tensing our muscles in an effort to control the intensity of discharge.)

I often wonder, is it possible that we never would be associating crying with pain if from our births onward we had consistently received such warm, accepting, and patient attention for crying that we usually cried when we needed to and therefore never had any reason to associate crying with pain. Yes, I wonder. Might we never have associated emotional discharge with pain? My guess: yes. Crying would mean relief, renewed optimism, and zest for life, love, and friendship.

If you are new to emotional discharge practice you will have to accept the fact that crying hurts every time, at least briefly. Strangely, once we have gained confidence in our ability to use the process and have stopped resisting discharge the hurt then begins to feel right and good. (I think we can thank evolution/Creation for that.)

CHAPTER 26

DEPROGRAMMING #2—TO ACTIVATE AND USE THE PROCESS IS <u>YOUR</u> GENUINE ACCOMPLISHMENT—SO GO FOR IT!

If you hadn't ridden a bike for thirty years but at the request of your granddaughter jumped on her mountain bike and cycled down a steep dirt path, would you consider that an accomplishment?   I hope so. (I certainly won't dare try anything like that until I have a gyroscope embedded somewhere in my body!)

Here's another type of accomplishment:

<u>the skillful discharge of emotion after thirty years of suppression.</u>

Yes, accomplishment!   Why would we believe that regaining the ability to successfully discharge emotion was anything other than a major accomplishment?   If our brains naturally *want* to do it and it improves our ability to not only cope with the stressful demands of life but find more pleasure and meaning in our lives, and we regain our ability to do it, then—

Emotional discharge is a MAJOR accomplishment.

When I was first introduced to the practice of emotional discharge I had no clue that crying over anything (or over nothing consequential) was going to impact my life the way it did. Surely, not! But I did believe that I was accomplishing something every time that I cried because I always felt good afterwards. I urge you to adopt the same belief—emotional discharge is an accomplishment as significant as any accomplishment a person can think of.

Do you want to know how strongly I felt about crying's value to me when I was first learning to *allow* emotion with tears? I carried all of my wet soggy tissues home with me and stored them in supermarket paper bags stacked in the closet! Sometimes I would count the tissues and tell my best friend, "That was a *(insert number)* tissue session." I stacked bags for several years then forgot about them. When decades later I did find them in the attic, I vividly recalled how grateful I felt for every tissue I used. (Recently, I enjoyed a four-tissue exchange with a fellow practitioner.)

Speaking of accomplishments, I want you to know that I don't choose to take credit for my well-being. I give credit to the process. It is the process that rescued me; it is the process that accomplished my liberation from the unpredictability of depression/mood swings. I have merely provided the will to *do it* and been, therefore, enormously fortunate. I think it is time for you to be fortunate, too.

One more thing—have you at all wondered why I call the natural process of emotional discharge a practice? I do so because we learn to intentionally activate the process with discipline, efficiency and effectiveness, on a relatively regular schedule.

That is the definition of a practice.

CHAPTER 27

HOW I HAVE USED THE PROCESS TO BUST STRESS

Here are six examples of how, in my daily life, I have used emotional discharge to bust stress.

<u>EXAMPLE #1:</u>

Recently, while driving home from the post office I suddenly worried about something and then got angry at myself because I had failed to be conscientious about dealing with it. I started to feel pressure in my throat and jaw so I said loudly, twice, in an angry voice, "I want to get rid of this!" By speaking with force I utilized those tense throat and jaw muscles so that I felt some relief, but I knew I needed a lot more relief. I then immediately asked myself, "Who do I want to talk to?"

I said the very first thought that next came to mind, "Mother, I need to discharge," and burst into tears. I repeated those words aloud until no more tears came. The throat tension had vanished.

What you may not have guessed—my mom had died. That was not a problem. I *talk* to a lot of deceased family members during discharge efforts and I do not expect them to hear me nor do I try to imagine that they are with me in the car. We are *designed* to communicate. If we listen carefully to the tone, pitch, inflection, and volume of our own voices we actually <u>are</u> attentively communicating; we are attentively communicating with ourselves.

EXAMPLE #2

While in church recently I experienced a number of powerful surges of emotion. I could have sobbed up a river or ocean but I controlled myself *the skillful emotionality* way; during each surge I took a slow, deep breath which greatly reduced the intensity. Without embarrassment, I allowed tears to flow down my cheeks. (They tickled.) Did I get a little stressed out while in church? No, I was relaxed throughout the service because I made no effort to control my emotions. To control my emotions I would have had to tense muscles; not one muscle was tensed; no stress.

EXAMPLE #3

Over thirty years ago, as I was driving from Rutland, Vermont, to Glastonbury, Connecticut, I began obsessing on one of my very old and dangerous thoughts. I called a fellow practitioner of emotional discharge to see if she had any time to do an exchange of attention. I told her that a thought was really scaring me.

Fortunately for me, she was available. Soon we were sitting in her small kitchen. We set a timer for thirty minutes (exchanges are timed) and I went first. Her attention was so warm and unworried, and I was so upset, that I easily cried up a storm (two tornadoes and a hurricane) and in less than ten minutes I was, for the time being, obsession-free. I don't remember if I told her exactly what I was thinking but perhaps I did. You will discover that you don't have to disclose what you are thinking in order to activate the process; you simply have to <u>silently think</u> the emotion-activating thought(s).

From that particular experience I learned that discharge can, in a sense, detach emotion(s) from a disturbing thought. Without the fuel of emotion(s), the thought and the desires associated with it can't be sustained. In short, under certain circumstances obsessions will not survive discharge.

As I drove home I began to worry that the obsession had already returned. So, to find out if I truly was safe from it I forced myself to think the thought. Oh, the relief! It no longer was accompanied by any feelings or emotion. I <u>was</u> safe. There was no emotion to make me want to act on it. That was a reassuring discovery. Ultimately, I deactivated the obsession completely. How I did that is a short long story not for this book..

EXAMPLE #4

Over thirty-five years ago, when I was driving home in the dark after an evening class where we had practiced emotional discharge with partners, I ran over an opossum. Because I had just left a training class where emotionality was prized <u>and</u> practiced and because I had, as usual, discharged up a few tornadoes, I instantly burst into scalding tears of anger and grief.   Jamming on the brakes, I leaped out of the car and with a flashlight hunted for the corpse.   Instead of a corpse I found the flattened end of the opossum's tail and no opossum.   Tremendously relieved, I returned to the car...and cried myself home.   It was twenty solid minutes of bawling like a baby because my brain was reactivating memories of animals I had lost. (Trust your brain to use a present moment to heal old hurts!)   By the time I pulled in the driveway I had stopped crying; I was de-stressed.   I was sad, too.   The opossum had lost the end of its tail.   (At the time it didn't occur to me that the opossum must have been terrified and in terrible pain.)

Once in the house I encountered Sweet Boy the Cat. Naturally, I leaned down to stroke his large white body...and was stunned: I felt not only fur but muscles. I also felt how solid, how dense and heavy, his fine feline body was. A realization hit me like a ton of concrete blocks—before this moment I had never felt anything but fur or feathers for any animal that I had touched. Somehow, the heavy heartfelt crying over the opossum and my pet animals had re-established a lost ability, a lost tactile connection to an animal.   (Emotional discharge doesn't only bust stress.   It often provides us with unexpected additional benefits.   Be ready.)

EXAMPLE #5

In all these years I never really thought about using emotional discharge to eliminate fatigue, but not too long ago I learned it can.   I was scheduled to do an exchange of attention with my friend, John, and I was so tired that I was certain I would fall asleep during his time if not during my own.   I told him that.   He suggested that I go first anyway.   I thought to myself, unhappily, "Boy, I'm going to fall asleep when he takes his turn."

Only I did not fall asleep during his turn because I woke up completely during my own.   While thinking out loud I struck gold: a thought that activated a flood of tears.   I have no recollection what that thought was but I squeezed every bit of emotion out of it and then said to him, in genuine awe, "I don't believe this, but I'm totally awake!" I looked down at the soggy tissues I'd dropped on the floor and said, "Wow, I woke up on a six-tissue discharge."

EXAMPLE #6

Oh, I now need to add one more example.

Recently, I began a chore that for two reasons I had put off for over a year.   It was mopping a floor.   Floor mopping reminded me of my beloved grandparents, their guest lodge, Pioneer Lodge, at Lake Bomoseen, Castleton,

110

Vermont, and my mom and dad. Sadness. But not only sadness! Frustration. I was feeling sorry for myself. I was feeling stress. I said to myself, "I've got to cry a little." Picturing the lake, the lodge, and my brother in his red and white second hand motor boat, I cried...and mopped. It wasn't long before the tears stopped. I no longer felt stressed.

I highly recommend that you learn how to cry while you do things you don't want to do or find difficult to do. If you are a professional procrastinator like me, this ability comes in handy.

CHAPTER 28

LET'S THINK ABOUT GETTING THE RIGHT KIND OF HELP #1

We don't have to go it alone. We can reach out for help! I have already told you that I will, if life becomes too stressful, and I promise you this:

I will NOT be looking for talk therapy!

Getting help is a brilliant thing to do and we deserve the right kind of help. By chance, not design, I always connected up with therapists who agreed to remain silent while I discharged emotion. Only when I had completed what I call the discharge cycle (explained later) did they then comment, guide, etc.

You may or may not know this, but there are psychotherapists and psychiatrists who are trained to provide some form of *emotion-centered* or *emotion-focused* therapy. Many of these individuals base their therapeutic approach on discoveries made by those doing research in the relatively new field named *affective neuroscience,* an interdisciplinary field that encompasses affective neuroscience (emotion and the brain), cognitive neuroscience, and the psychological study of personality, emotion, mood, and human relationships/connection.

Those two terms, *emotion-centered* and *emotion-focused*, can mean different things to different people, however. You will be best served by a professional who not only understands the value of emotional discharge and can remain attentive and silent while you discharge but who also will be able to recognize those moments when you need to discharge but don't realize it and will know how to direct your attention and provide guidance in those instances.   Individuals trained in emotion-centered therapy should be able to do that.   (All skilled therapists will help you talk about the thoughts, ideas, images, etc., and memories that arise during and after emotional discharge.)

When you speak with your potential therapist, make it clear that you need to stop being afraid of your feelings and emotions and the only way you can do that is by allowing yourself to experience them through crying.   Be blunt.   Ask, "Will you help me do that?"

If you learn to practice skillful emotionality (nothing more than crying on demand, your demand) you will never be totally dependent on the expertise of your therapist because you will be learning how to use the discharge skills in Part Four, and you can even teach your mental health professional how to help you use them.   I know that you can do that because that is what I did.

Training your therapist is easy! Select your favorite and most effective skills and tell them to use the skills with you. For example, I told my therapist that answering the question, "Who do I need to talk to," really worked well. So, he would ask me that question when he recognized my need to look at how I was feeling.

Occasionally, timing his words well, he would ask me, "What do you wish that *they* would say to you?" That was his technique; I must tell you, it really was a good one! He was a really skilled therapist! His specialty was Gestalt Therapy. It is worth investigating.

CHAPTER 29

WHY NOT ABANDON THESE TWO LEARNED DESENSITIZING THOUGHTS <u>TODAY</u>

When it comes to emotion and emotionality, desensitization is the process that occurs as we gradually learn how to ignore, discount, deny, and/or bury our feelings and emotions.

So what is desensitization? It is *reduced emotional responsiveness to stimuli*. When social programming *works*, we gradually become desensitized to a lot:

1. to inherently upsetting emotion-evoking stimuli—for example, the sight of a frightened, starving, sick, injured, or dead human or animal or the death of trees—they all are so magnificent.
2. to the stimuli of our own physical sensations, in particular to those sensations that naturally occur and also signal the availability of emotion. You read about the sensations in Chapter 8: *The **Big Reveal** and Deprogramming #1*.
3. to the stimuli of our own thoughts. Thoughts that normally would activate emotion when we focus our attention on them no longer do.

4. to stimuli consisting of the sound of our own voices as we talk or weep. One of our important skills requires focusing attention on the sound of our own voices, and until we are able to tolerate hearing ourselves some of us listen to heart pumping loud music so that we can't hear our voices at all.

Now, this is the chapter where I encourage you to eliminate two emotion-desensitizing thoughts that we typically learn from adults and then pass on, like viruses, to others. Both of these thoughts contribute to the desensitization process by minimizing the importance of painful incidents so that painful emotional reactions and outward expression of distress are judged unnecessary, unjustified, and unjustifiable.

Be on guard for the following two automatic thoughts which often arise when something that is upsetting occurs:

1. *just a*. For example, "It was *just a* mouse I ran over." Or, "Well, *just a* few people died." Or, "Don't get upset because that's *just a*..," (you complete the sentence).

2. *it doesn't really matter*. If something evokes emotional distress and pain for you or for someone in your company, it really matters. In our society we learn that so many things don't matter one is almost tempted to conclude that nothing matters, which is exactly what some of us do, but everything

matters, really. We discover this as we bust stress and refine our ability to use the discharge process. Once we are able to regularly discharge intense emotion we see more clearly the consequences of our own actions and of the actions others, including of governments and nations, and we truly understand that everything matters and we cannot abide suffering, at all. (Do not assume that I am doing much to reduce suffering, however. The unhappy truth is, I am only writing this book and being as supportive of family and friends as I can be; and they are doing the same for me.)

Listen for *just a* and *it doesn't matter* when spoken by either you or others. Know that both phrases allow suffering, often enormous suffering, to continue unnecessarily.

Growing up I heard those words at times. I learned them and even said them to myself. But thinking those words now is no option for me since they would permit me to avoid painful emotion, in short, ignore Reality. I never want to do that again. **Don't forget...**

crying is natural.

It's NOT CRYING that is unnatural.

Two anecdotes are called for here.

Anecdote #1: Decades ago my mom and I were enjoying a Sunday drive in central Vermont near Middlebury College, her alma mater. It was a sunny day. We were peaceful and content until a mouse ran into the road and my mom ran over it. Horrified and heartbroken, I cried out, "Mother, you could have saved it." She replied, "Pam, I didn't have time. It was just a mouse." I heard self-defense as well as sorrow in her voice. I really did hear those feelings. But I got mad anyway and said something. Maybe I said this, with a mini-snarl, "You could have jerked the wheel."

It did not occur to me to comfort her, of course. The range of emotions that I was capable of noticing and responding to at that time was still quite limited. Hearing pain and instantly wanting to comfort was not yet one of my automatic empathic responses. I wish that I had comforted her, however; my mom truly loved and respected all animals.

Anecdote #2: Not long ago I was driving back from church with my friend, Wes, who, like me, loves animals. Although we were driving beside a small river frequented by adorable (to me) opossums and other small animals and I should have been alert, I was not watching the road carefully. Suddenly, he said in a mildly accusing voice, "You just ran over a baby turtle." Instantly, I felt sad and also guilty about my inattention; probably I was admiring

118

the boulders in the brook beside me because I love rocks of any size.

I felt an impulse to defend myself. Instead, I said, "Oh, no!" An instant replay of the words my mom had heard me say to her decades earlier prompted me to shut my mouth rather than defensively point out that the turtle was small and nearly the color of the pavement and besides, "It was just a turtle." Instead of defending myself as there was no defense, I repeated, "Oh, no," and <u>forced</u> myself to notice feelings of sorrow and regret. I knew that I should discharge eventually on that split-millisecond impulse to not care about the turtle's life.

Some well-meaning people who are unaware of the high cost of avoiding emotional pain, might say, with kind intention, "That's unwise. That is past. You must focus on the present if you want to avoid depression/mood swings." I would respond, "I understand your reasoning, but by taking this impulse seriously I <u>am</u> focusing on the present and I will be preparing for the future, too." This is what I mean—reality has provided me with evidence that the impulse to avoid emotional pain still exists. I intend to eliminate that impulse just as I have eliminated depression and mood swings in my life. If I don't eventually eliminate the impulse to avoid painful feelings/emotions I then remain at risk of failing to act with love and compassion in the future when I encounter pain and suffering. Not only that, I will fail to bust stress.

Because our brains respond emotionally to all stimuli, internal and external, and because stress results when stimuli trigger tension and pain that we fail to discharge, stress will result; really, our brains and bodies, which constantly exchange information, are that precise.

When we have low tolerance for painful emotion it is all too easy for us to ignore, discount, deny, and bury the feelings that we naturally have when our actions harm or kill any form of life, and every conscious decision that we make to avoid experiencing empathic pain for another form of life further desensitizes us. Let's not settle for an unending continuation of this desensitization process that endangers all that we love in Life.

Wes did offer words of comfort when he saw that I was upset. I don't recall what he said but I was luckier than my mom had been because he was emotionally supportive. Yup, I was luckier. Don't you agree?

CHAPTER 30

A HUMANE MISSION: RE-EDUCATE HUMANITY—MILLIONAIRES AND BILLIONAIRES WELCOME!

It might be a little early in your reading for me to introduce this idea, but I am providing it now, nevertheless.   I have no idea what you may think of it.

Worldwide, humans are having a disastrous time. Already, I have stated the obvious, that very little will become easier or better for most of humanity.   Global warming, which many of us deny <u>only</u> because our wealth/income depends on activities that contribute to it, is going to put at risk the welfare of all living beings presently surviving.   However, our species possesses, and will possess, tools psychological, technological, and spiritual that <u>may</u> reduce or eliminate suffering—and also save us and many of Earth's nonhuman residents.

Emotional discharge is a *tool* with many physical *features*, uses, and effects on us and on our societies...when we use it (or don't use it).   I hope that I have convinced you, *humanity needs to wrestle this stress-busting process out of the toolbox because empathy and compassion are natural outcomes of emotional discharge*, and only empathy and compassion will motivate us to help everyone rather than a select few, and inspire us, also, to rescue our precious planet.

How do we get crying out of the toolbox and *back into* the brain? How do we re-educate and train an entire planet of human beings who desperately need this process? What would a worldwide campaign or public education program utilizing every available form of technology look like?"

I'm not sure what it would *look* like but I know some of the things that we will need.

<u>The Citizens' Campaign</u>

To promote the process, those of us who wish to participate in the campaign will:

1. design, produce, and sell all kinds of useless but decorative, or useful and eye-catching, products that advertise the process, all to be sold in every venue we can think of, for personal financial gain (money!). Ethics, morality, and wisdom must rule.
2. produce and sell original art and music that arouses curiosity and inspires experimentation with the practice, for personal financial gain (money!). Ethics, morality, and wisdom must rule.
3. write and sell informative and fascinating books, magazines, newsletters, and mini-newspapers that will be available online and offline, for personal

financial gain (money!).   Ethics, morality, and wisdom must rule.

4. develop and present online and offline educational programs that include demonstrations of skillful emotionality (emotional discharge).   Ethics, morality, and wisdom must rule.

5. organize practice support groups that govern themselves and pay nothing to outside entities. Ethics, morality, and wisdom must rule.

6. convene hubs where people can get together and share ideas and resources and also practice together if they wish.   Ethics, morality, and wisdom must rule.

The Millionaire/Billionaires' Campaign

We will need hundreds of (compulsively?) generous and compassionate millionaires and billionaires (you?) to devote thousands and millions, maybe billions, of dollars to fund:

1. the production of eye catching, motivating, and inspirational *educational* infomercials and advertising designed for all platforms.
2. the launching and financing of at least one exciting and stimulating educational,

multi-lingual multi-faceted *magazine* promoting the practice of emotional discharge.
3. parent-education-and-training programs where <u>all participants receive wages</u>.
4. education/training classes for humans of all ages held in clubs, schools, places of worship and spirituality, senior centers, town halls, etc., where <u>all participants earn a wage</u>.
5. funding for current schools and campuses to establish and maintain education/training classes where <u>all participants receive wages</u>.
6. funding for the establishment of new and free trade schools and colleges where emotional discharge and other healthful practices are an integral part of the curriculum and <u>where all participants in training classes will receive wages.</u>

Maybe this is a ridiculous idea.   Maybe this is a monumental task.   It might be both, so let's get started right now...**by practicing ourselves**. **This means YOU.**

If you are wealthy or you have any spare change, will you help?   If so, find some entrepreneurs who with your $$$ will begin *production* NOW!

PART TWO

SELF-EXAMINATION

What is going to prevent YOU from using emotional discharge to bust stress when you need to?

LET'S FIND OUT!

Please, jump ahead to the sections on skillful emotionality or on mood swings if the pace of this book is too slow for you.

CHAPTER 31

WHAT DO <u>YOU</u> REALLY THINK?

I hope that you have been jumping ahead in your reading whenever you began to get bored, were overcome by curiosity *(what are these skills??),* or were attacked by doubt *(come on, emotional discharge can't be this good!!).* If you feel compelled to jump ahead right now, I beg you, do so. Then, eventually, return to this section. Know your enemies, the socially programmed assumptions, attitudes, beliefs, and values that will limit your access to this stress-busting process

TRY TO NOTICE AND EVEN WRITE DOWN YOUR VERY FIRST THOUGHTS AND/OR FEELINGS/EMOTIONS.

CHAPTER 32

A MINI-QUESTIONNAIRE

1. If you were to begin crying or tearing up at this very moment, what thoughts about yourself would arise?

2. If someone you know or love began to cry or had tears in their eyes, what thoughts about them would arise?

3. Are you able to cry with tears?

4. In your lifetime, who have you seen cry? (If you must maintain privacy, use initials or your own code.)

5. Who have you seen cry and in doing so receive emotional support?

6. Who have you seen cry and receive the reverse: punishment, belittling, shaming, maybe even worse?

7.   Was there ever a time when you started to cry and stopped yourself?

8.   Did you ever want to cry but didn't?   If the answer is yes, why didn't you?

8.   Have you ever stopped anyone else from crying?   If the answer is yes, what did you say or do in order to accomplish your objective?

9.   When you have cried has anyone ever tried to comfort you with pats or hugs?

CHAPTER 33

YOUR SENTENCE-COMPLETION EXAM

What do *you* believe about crying and laughing with tears? Complete the following sentences with <u>all the first few thoughts</u> that arise.   Brainstorm on this.   Do it with a friend, even.

1. Crying with tears is:

2. Children who cry are:

3. Adults who cry are:

4. Crying is acceptable in these situations:

5. Crying is not acceptable in these situations.

5. Laughing with tears is:

6. Adults who laugh with tears are:

7. If I cry with tears I think that I am:

8. If I laugh with tears I think that I am:

9. If I were with someone who began to cry I would say:

CHAPTER 34

YOUR TRUE-FALSE TEST

To the best of your ability, write your <u>immediate</u> reaction to each item below. **DO NOT THINK!** Remember, this self-examination will help you identify the embedded and automatic beliefs, assumptions, attitudes, and values that will interfere with your ability to regain use of the process. This process might save your life so it is important to understand the *forces* <u>aligned against you</u>.

The word *laughing* is for the most part omitted here but we know that laughing frequently alternates with crying. In order for <u>natural, unconstrained emotional discharge</u> to occur we must eventually become comfortable with this alternation since laughter reduces tension. If we prevent ourselves from laughing, we interfere with the spontaneous unfolding of our thoughts, memories, feelings, and emotions. That is our goal: <u>the spontaneous unfolding of our thoughts, memories, feelings, and emotions</u>. Our poor beleaguered brains are blocked from thinking clearly at nearly every turn, it can seem. What do I mean? To avoid emotionality, we block the natural transmission of information within our brains, sending the signals instead, with distractions, in all directions (figuratively speaking, of course).

How can we accurately perceive and interpret reality under those circumstances? We can't do that, which means decisions we make may not be as constructive as we think they will be. (Look at the decisions promoted/made by those with political influence and power. Neuroscience has proved that political decisions we make are based on emotion despite our assumption that our decisions and also the decisions of others are based on facts, information, and logic, only.) So, begin this test now!

T = True
F = False

1. Once children begin crying, they should then stop crying as soon as they can.
2. Parents should always help their children avoid crying.
3. Parents should always help their children stop crying if they can't stop themselves.
4. Distraction is the best way to stop children from crying.
5. As they get older, children should learn not to cry except in certain situations.
6. Once people are teenagers they should have gained enough control of themselves to avoid crying most if not all of the time, except in certain situations.

7. Healthy teenagers hardly ever have any reason to cry.
8. It's natural to look down on teenagers who cry.
9. People who are depressed cry too much.
10. People who are depressed don't cry enough.
11. People who are high cry too much.
12. People who are high have no need to cry.
13. When people cry they usually feel worse afterwards.
14. Some people don't cry often enough.
15. Some people cry too often.
16. Some people don't cry as hard as they really need to.
17. Once people begin to cry they usually can't stop.
18. People who cry lack self-control.
19. People who cry are weak.
20. Crying is pointless.
21. Crying wastes time.
22. Few adults have a need to cry.
23. Crying is self-indulgence.
24. Crying so that others see us is selfish as it brings the others down, makes them feel bad.
25. People cry only to get sympathy.
26. No one cries in front of other people unless they want to influence how the other people feel about or treat them.
27. Crying is usually an attempt to manipulate others.
28. People who let themselves cry in front of others usually are trying to get sympathy.

29. If we feel self-pity we should NEVER let ourselves cry.
30. There are no health benefits to crying.
31. It's unhealthy to cry then laugh then cry then laugh.
32. Crying is disgusting to see.
33. Men shouldn't cry much if at all.
34. Men don't need to cry as much as women do.
35. People who cry in public lose respect whatever their age.
36. People who cry on their job often lose their jobs.
37. It's natural to hear a joke and laugh so hard that you get tears in your eyes.
38. When we laugh till we cry it means nothing.
39. Truly healthy people don't benefit much from crying unless, for example, there's been a death or serious loss.
40. There's no way that crying could make learning new things easier.

There, you just finished glancing at, or carefully completing, a mini-questionnaire, a sentence completion exam, and a true/false test. These were provided so that you could become more aware of the programming you received while you were growing up.

Now that you know what you are up against, plan to reverse that programming so you can bust stress, prevent depression, and eliminate "harmful" mood swings..

PART THREE

THE PRACTICE OF SKILLFUL EMOTIONALITY

CHAPTER 35

WHAT THE HECK IS *SKILLFUL EMOTIONALITY?*

What is this stress-busting practice that I love to do alone and also, by utilizing the simple attention-exchange format described below, with others. Sure, the name suggests what it is, but...well, this is it whether practiced alone or in good company: ***skillful emotionality* is a practice and discipline involving the skillful (fast and effective) activation and (fearless) discharge of emotion.**

Practicing Alone

Because our stress management goal is to keep stress minimal, we take the time, daily, to notice how stressed or relaxed we feel. Then, if we are disciplined (I do not claim to always be disciplined), whether or not we consciously feel stress or distress we check our own mental states by using one or more of the emotion-activating skills listed further in the book.

When I am alone in my car my favorite *skills* are questions that I silently ask myself:

1. Who do I want to talk to?
2. What do I need to say?

136

If my Dad's name comes instantly to mind I do not wonder if I really want to talk to him; I take that first thought seriously and immediately say out loud , "Dad," and then say loudly my very first thoughts...which can be anything. If the thoughts that arise trigger emotion, I allow emotional discharge.   My loving dad is dead, of course, and we never had a relationship because early in my childhood I locked him out of my mind.   That definitely is one of my deepest regrets!

The other discharge skill that I depend on involves giving thanks, i.e., *doing gratitudes.*   If I am in my car, such a quiet sanctuary for stress busting and self-exploration, and I slowly say aloud the names of each of my deceased family members and relatives, I usually recall their acts of love and kindness that I hardly appreciated while they were alive and I naturally feel deep regret and sadness.   If there is stress, the tears really flow, I am relieved, and I thank them for all that they did for me.   I also thank Reality and Creation for giving me the opportunity to become aware of my omissions and commissions.

Practicing with Others

Some of us love to hike, some of us to play computer games, some of us to travel or ride horseback or volunteer

137

with animal rescue organizations. I love to practice skillful emotionality with my fellow human beings. When a comrade leaks (or bursts into) tears and sheds stress like it's a coat of heavy armor, I am so **so** relieved and happy for them that I could cry (but don't as it would distract them), and to be in the presence of those learning how to emotionally connect with one another and use warm attention to bust stress—what joy. I can't describe how I feel when a partner has most obviously set the goal of (1) discharge without limits and (2) no boundaries to Reality and truth! It is beyond joy.

The Format

Most people hearing about the group practice of skillful emotionality ask if someone leads the group or acts as facilitator. The answer is: no. Why is no leader or facilitator necessary? One reason is: exchanges of attention are timed and the mechanical or digital timer, or stopwatch, rules. Another reason is: it is essential that we all take full charge of learning to use specific skills that help us focus our attention so that we can activate emotion.

I believe that this format works well for nearly everyone because:

1. each person has an <u>equal period of time</u> to give attention as well as receive and use attention—all

without the stress (and distraction) of being interrupted by others' questions, comments, or suggestions and guidance.

2. we evenly divide the time available for the exchange... no one is favored.
3. each of us is responsible for promptly stopping our talking or emotional discharge when our time is up.
4. each of us is in charge of how we use our time.
5. each of us learns the skills of emotion activation and emotional discharge so no one needs to prompt or guide us; we guide ourselves toward emotionality.
6. when the exchange of attention is over, when everyone has had time, no one comments or asks us questions unless we have stated that it is then okay to do so.

I found learning to stop on time, even when I was in the middle of something intense, to be empowering. I guess that knowing I was personally responsible for stopping on time evoked a sense of freedom and independence. Does that sound strange? All I can say is, during my initial brain retraining efforts it was this requirement that I manage my own time which gave me the self-confidence to relinquish control of my emotions.

The equal-time no-interruption format really has always worked for me. I never have to worry about being interrupted if I pause to think, review memories, *watch* images, or discharge emotion. I know that no one will inadvertently dominate the exchange? I feel safe knowing that during my time there won't be any cross-talk, conversation, or discussion and certainly no questions or interpretations of what I talk about?

Some of you will find it easier to *allow* the process when you are alone. Some of you will find it easier when you are not alone and are receiving at least one person's attention, in person or by phone, etc. I am able to easily access the process both when I am alone and when I am with others. Eventually, you will learn to be just as re-sensitized to emotion and to attention as I am. I promise that!

I do believe that most of us, including those of us who are accustomed to discharging alone, benefit **HUGELY** from exchanging attention with one or more people. This is because few of us receive adequate high quality attention either for noticing our thoughts and feelings or for reflection with emotion. Science has proved that attention stimulates the brain. Infants and babies require attention for brain development and psychological maturation. We require it, too, for everything. So please don't write off exchanges. You deserve to know what they have to offer you.

Next, a little poem I forgot that I wrote just for all of us.

We don't know we're feeling lonely (exchange lonely
with word appropriate for how you feel).

We think we're feeling fine.

But once we have attention

our emotions fall out in line.

Grief, fear, rage, love...

Each one deserves our time.

They <u>ALL</u> are fine.

CHAPTER 36

SKILLFUL EMOTIONALITY—A PRACTICE WITH OPTIONS!

Is it not useful to have at least one health practice that can be done in a wide variety of situations? I bet we both think so. We can safely use the process of emotional discharge alone or with others while—

- sitting down. I do.
- walking and running. I do.
- swimming (but not underwater). I have.
- talking on the phone. I have.
- listening to music. I have.
- composing music, doing art.
- reading, writing, or journaling. I do.
- performing in plays and participating in improvs.
- driving (my favorite setting when I am alone).

There are other options, of course, such as practicing in the presence of a trusted professional. I practiced skillful emotionality with a pastoral counselor, a social worker, a psychologist, and a psychiatrist. At one point in my life I was seeing three professionals at the same time. These individuals gave me silent attention while I *tracked down* thoughts that evoked emotion. My intention to discharge enabled my excellent brain to uncover emotion-rich First Thoughts. With intention, you will be able to reliably do the same and while discharging you will bust stress like crazy, which means, fast and thoroughly.

DISCHARGE

TO

RECHARGE!

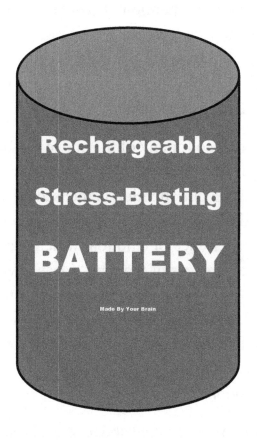

CHAPTER 37

PURPOSES FOR WHICH SKILLFUL EMOTIONALITY IS NOT PRACTICED

Skillful emotionality is not practiced:

1. to influence or manipulate the behavior of another person.
2. to attract the attention of others or to gain their approval or support.
3. to receive sympathy or pity.
4. to win relief from stress at another's expense.
5. to entertain our listeners.

When we practice for any of the above reasons we lose out. How is that possible? The answer is, *distraction*. In each instance our attention is focused on the behavior (actions and reactions) of others rather than on our own conscious experience of emotion, which is so essential, and on our awareness of thoughts, ideas, memories, and images, etc., that arise. Because of distraction we fail to become independently skillful; so, when we are alone and need to bust stress we are unable to easily select the most effective skills for the moment and quickly and effectively activate emotion.

In the fourth instance noted above, *to win relief from stress at another's expense*, we not only are distracted, we undermine and even damage our relationships which ultimately produces rather than reduces stress.

In the fifth instance, *to interest or entertain anyone*, we not only are distracted by our efforts to determine the effect we are having on our listeners, we are preventing ourselves from being real. **When we practice skillful emotionality we should NEVER try to be interesting or entertaining. Never! Never! Never!** We must be real and accurate when we report our feelings, emotions, thoughts, memories, etc.

If we grew up feeling that we had to earn or win attention by being interesting, by entertaining, or by being useful in some way, for example, by providing information or assuming an educator role, we will find it a challenge to ignore the compulsion or temptation to do so. We may, therefore, only talk. Or we might in some way provide a performance. Either way, we will not activate emotional discharge and bust stress. Don't talk if you want to bust stress. Use the discharge skills!

There is one more issue I have not mentioned yet. It concerns your partner(s). They need you to be as *genuine* as you can be. They deserve to be in the company of the real 100% genuine you.

CHAPTER 38

LIST OF SKILLS FOR THE ATTENTION-USER

Twelve skills are listed here. Don't worry; there's nothing to remember! Beginners: when you intend to discharge emotion you simply hold the list in your hands and *try out* each skill to find out which one(s) activate emotion. Each of us experiments. Eventually, as long as you really focus your attention on the skills, you will find a dependable skill combination and no longer need any list. I already told you what my favorite skills are: *who do I need to talk to*; *what do I need to say*; and, *gratitudes*.

Do keep the following statement in mind for yourself:

emotional discharge is good for everyone, including ME!

It is your job, and opportunity, to select the right skill for the moment. If you feel stuck and have a partner you or your partner can read the list of skills out loud. Notice sensations, feelings, thoughts. Chances are, one skill may instantly appeal. Use it promptly. For easy reference, here is your abbreviated, but complete, list. (You may add to the list, of course. Trust your brain.) A detailed list follows this first list.

SKILL#1—DEPROGRAMMING: <u>remind yourself</u> that any inaccurate(*negative*) thoughts/beliefs/attitudes that you have about discharge were learned and are not in any way justified. Emotional discharge has enormous stress-busting value and you deserve to receive its benefits.

SKILL #2—ATTENTION: sense and use attention.

SKILL #3—BODY: sense your body.

SKILL #4—FIRST THOUGHTS: watch for and say first thoughts.

SKILL #5—VOICE: listen to, and use, your voice.

SKILL #6—BODY: use your body

SKILL #7—REPETITION: repeat silently or aloud anything that seems to activate emotion.

SKILL #8—BE DRAMATIC, EXAGGERATE.

SKILL #9—REPORT EMOTION: wave or say *emotion* in monotone or name the emotion.

SKILL #10—KEY QUESTIONS:

    ☐ What am I thinking/feeling right now?
    ☐ What do I need to say right now?
    ☐ What's difficult or hard for me right now?

☐ What encouraging words do I need to hear right now?

SKILL #11—WHO DO I NEED TO TALK TO?
WHAT DO I NEED TO SAY TO THEM?

SKILL #12—THE GRATITUDES—what am I thankful or grateful for?

NOTE: It is always okay to be intentionally silly.

CHAPTER 39

SKILLS FOR THE ATTENTION-USER, IN DETAIL

Reminder: it is always okay to be intentionally silly.

SKILL #1—DEPROGRAMMING: ELIMINATE ALL UNHELPFUL THINKING ABOUT THE VALUE OF EMOTIONAL DISCHARGE

You already know that your programmed, unhelpful thinking will interfere with your ability to access this stress-busting process. Therefore your assumptions and beliefs (influencing your attitudes and viewpoints) about emotional discharge must become the focus of your number one *skill*. When you notice programmed, unhelpful thoughts about the process arising, immediately replace (counteract or reverse) them. For example, if you find yourself thinking, "Only weak cowards cry," reverse that: "Only strong heroes cry."

You can practice this skill at any time by simply reminding yourself, off and on during your day, **"It is good and wise to allow emotion if it is there."**

Once we become skilled, nothing interferes with our ability to use the process. We notice emotion; we *allow* it. We notice stress. We look for a thought that will activate emotion.

Whatever doubts you may have regarding your ability to reclaim the process as your own, I assure you, you can reclaim everything, yes, everything. Yes, at first you may want to have a warm, encouraging, and confident counselor as an assistant, and all I can say is, "Go for it." As you know, I used professional help for years and it was worth it!

SKILL #2—Intermittently, deeply SENSE THE ATTENTION you are receiving

The brain is designed to discharge emotion. Warm and focused attention is a catalyst. For the catalyst to work we need to feel, or sense, attention. To do this, intermittently focus your attention on your listeners' eyes and intend to **CONSCIOUSLY SEE THEM SEEING YOU**. Do this at times while talking and discharging emotion. Whenever you notice you've stopped talking or discharging emotion, return your attention to their eyes and again intend to consciously see them seeing you. With practice you will be able to decide to see them seeing you while you are thinking, talking out loud, or discharging. When you can do that you will have perfected this skill.

Normally, of course, it never occurs to us to consciously try to see a listener seeing us. We look at our listeners to see if they are looking back at us or are looking in our eyes, but we don't deeply see them seeing us. I believe that developing this skill was critical, for me. Had I not practiced this skill I may never have discovered something that still boggles my mind. It happened years ago. While trying to use this skill in an exchange with a friend, I suddenly saw her seeing me and I thought, "My god, that never happened before." I was shocked, and I told her I suddenly could see her seeing and listening to me.

It was a precious experience that also was heartbreaking. Not only did I realize for the first time that I'd not been seeing my listeners and feeling their attention most of my life, I realized that I had never given anyone in my life truly aware attention because I wasn't really *seeing* them. That includes my loved ones, I am afraid.

I think my inability to feel attention makes sense. My mom had long ago told me that she had been depressed after my birth. Likely, it was post partum depression exacerbated by the fact that I was premature and in an incubator, not in her arms, for a period of time. Then there's my mom's vulnerability to depression.

Research has proved that parents who are depressed are unable, for the most part, to give consistent, predictable, focused and warm attention. Even infants and babies notice a lack of focused attention, which instinctively triggers alarm.   Perhaps, to avoid feeling alarmed, I learned not be aware of the lack of focused and warm attention and in order to do that I had to stop naturally sensing attention (personal explanation, only).

As practitioners of *skillful emotionality*, we call this *type* of attention, **DYNAMIC ATTENTION** as practiced and experienced by the attention-user.

SKILL #3—SENSE YOUR BODY

We have discussed the fact that our brain sends us messages in the form of physical sensations, telling us that emotion is available and emotional discharge would be useful.   As a skill, we try to be constantly aware of our body's sensations, positions, and movements.

This skill is called a *body scan* in the practice I began in 1974.   Those who practice a form of Buddhist meditation*, insight meditation*, or who learn Mindfulness Based Stress Reduction, MBSR, a stress-reduction program which I present in a little more detail later, name it *mindfulness of the body*.   To do a body scan we bring our attention to our body by focusing our full attention on it and intentionally checking, from foot to head (my preference) for the occurrence of physical sensations.

Sensations can be subtle and challenging to detect, gross and easy to detect, or impossible to ignore.   A person who has perfected the body scan is acutely aware, minute to minute and even second to second, of the wide range of physical sensations that the body generates. That is not all. The person notices, also, the thoughts, ideas, images, memories, feelings, in short, everything that arise in the mind, during the body scan. It may be hard to believe but during practice everything is worth noticing whether or not it seems important. Nothing is discounted. Anything might activate emotion.

The ability to consciously sense what is going on in our bodies is so essential for defeating depression and eliminating mood swings that I consider it an essential skill, an absolutely essential skill, and perfection requires discipline. In fact, this skill requires self-discipline. .

If you notice: tightness or stiffness of muscles including facial muscles; chills and tingles anywhere in your body including scalp; itching, aches and pains; and tickling sensations near the eyes, there is a good chance that what you just thought, remembered, or visualized had emotion associated with it, emotion that might become available for discharge. Try to recall whatever preceded the sensation. Review that silently or report aloud. _If emotion is evoked, **stop talking**, sense your body, allow emotional discharge, notice arising thoughts, and if any of the new thoughts activate emotion, sense your body, allow discharge, etc._

In order for you to discharge you may need to continuously relax your jaw and slightly separate your lips. When we consciously or unconsciously try to control our emotions we tighten muscles such as the jaw and lips. Relax both; discharge may ensue.

SKILL #4—WATCH FOR FIRST THOUGHTS

Always be on the alert for the first thought that comes to your mind even if you decide not to say it aloud. Voice first thoughts even when they seem ridiculous or unimportant and repeat first thoughts if you have an emotional or physical reaction to any of them. Be aware especially of thoughts that emerge before, during, and after *emotional discharge*. To gain the greatest stress-busting benefit, voice evocative thoughts repeatedly until no emotion discharge occur. First thoughts usually provide the pathway to emotional discharge.

SKILL #5—LISTEN TO AND USE YOUR VOICE

Constantly listen to your voice and use it as a tool of self-expression and tension release. Act immediately on impulses to speak energetically, dramatically, emphatically, loudly or softly, to sing, or to make noises of any type. Don't worry whether or not you make sense or startle anyone. Repeat whatever you said if you react, and employ all skills.

Speaking forcefully with emphasis and energy, which usually means speaking loudly, is one of my favorite skills. Those of us who learned as we grew up to inhibit ourselves often find this to be a rather scary skill. We can practice using our voices with fellow practitioners by taking turns saying loudly and forcefully selected words that aren't likely to restimulate anyone. Names of vegetables and fruit usually are *safe*. Imagine saying clearly and firmly *potato* and really noticing how it feels to speak in a strong voice!

It is entirely possible that someone will be restimulated by a *safe* word. That person, you or someone else (or me), will want to take the reaction to the word seriously. Five five minutes of attention from a partner or partners can be useful or the person can simple focus on the word during their actual *time*.

SKILL #6—USE YOUR BODY

You may want to use your body as a tool of self-expression and tension release. Act immediately on impulses to gesture, move your arms and legs, drum your feet, stand, jump straight up and down, change your position from standing to sitting or to lying down, etc. Report thoughts, memories, etc., and repeat if you discharge emotion.

When I have used attention I have often jumped up and down (for some reason) or flopped down on the floor.

155

SKILL #7—REPETITION

Always repeat the thought, words, and movements that precede, arise during, or follow emotional discharge until no discharge is activated. However, do this only if you are comfortable with prolonging discharge. Prolonging discharge can yield greater relief from stress and greater reduction in suffering. (However, prolonging discharge can also increase emotional intensity and bring subconscious thoughts, memories, etc., to the surface.)

SKILL #8—BE DRAMATIC, EXAGGERATE

Experiment with being dramatic, and exaggerate what you think and how feel. Use, and hear, your body and your voice.

SKILL #9—REPORT EMOTION

Depending on how comfortable you are with emotion, other than discharging you have three basic choices when you are not comfortable with emotionality. Each successive skill increases the likelihood that you will feel the feelings and consciously experience the emotion.

> Wave your hand if you sense or feel emotion.
> Say *emotion* in a monotone.
> Name the emotion in a monotone, i.e., say, "sadness."

You may wonder, why a monotone? Usually, by speaking in a monotone we are able to share information but avoid activating emotion.

I have used the monotone a lot in my adventures with skillful emotionality. Do not think you have to confine yourself to just a few words like naming an emotion.

SKILL #10—KEY QUESTIONS

You can always ask yourself the following questions out loud and answer them with your very FIRST THOUGHTS.

> What am I thinking/feeling right now?
> What do I need to say right now?
> What's difficult or hard for me right now?
> What encouraging words do I need to hear right now?

SKILL #11—WHO DO I NEED TO TALK TO? WHAT DO I NEED TO SAY TO THEM?

This is the skill that I always use first. I try another skill only if emotional discharge is not activated within a minute.

Ask yourself out loud, "Who do I need to talk to?" Address the first person whose name comes to mind. Then, tell them what you need to say. If emotion is not activated, repeat the name and what you already said or provide more details.

SKILL #12— THE GRATITUDES—what are you thankful or grateful for?

After asking yourself out loud, "Who do I need to talk to," say the person's name and then *thank that person in as much detail and as repeatedly, as you wish.* If discharge fails to ensue, select another person. Talk to as many people as you need to. Sometimes I list, aloud, everyone I want to thank. Reminiscing about at least one of the people always activates my emotions...and I should tell you this: I do not give thanks enough!)

CHAPTER 40

LIST OF SKILLS FOR THE ATTENTION-GIVER

For easy reference, here is the list of basic skills.

SKILL #1—INTEND TO GIVE ATTENTION WITH WARMTH, RESPECT, AND PATIENCE

SKILL #2—MAINTAIN DIRECT EYE CONTACT OR READINESS FOR DIRECT EYE CONTACT

SKILL #3—USE THE TINY SERENE SMILE

SKILL #4—REVIEW THE SKILLS TOGETHER

SKILL #5—WHAT ARE YOU THINKING?

CHAPTER 41

SKILLS FOR THE ATTENTION-GIVER, IN DETAIL

SKILL #1—INTEND TO GIVE ATTENTION WITH WARMTH, RESPECT, AND PATIENCE

By looking relaxed and interested, you will put your partner at ease. If you find yourself thinking less of them, or if you begin to feel impatient for any reason whatsoever, that is your social programming *mixed* with the treatment you received from others when you were talking or allowing emotion. It is good to be aware of your automatic thoughts and feelings/emotions.

You have promised to offer your best attention. So, as much as possible, don't think your own thoughts. Your mind will wander intermittently. Develop the skill of intending to notice when this happens so that you can refocus. You will eventually reach a point where you are not thinking at all when you listen. Your mind will be totally filled, every *space* of it, with them.

If occasionally, for a few split seconds, you have the feeling that you are looking directly into the mind of an amazing and precious loving intelligence, don't be astonished. That is what you <u>are</u> doing, and <u>you</u> are helping it liberate itself.

160

SKILL #2—MAINTAIN DIRECT EYE CONTACT

Your partner will look away from you often—while thinking, remembering, visualizing, and experiencing emotion. Always be ready for him/her to look directly back at you when you least expect it. Let your well-developed intuitive geometry tell you where to place your gaze so that when they unexpectedly look back at you, your eyes will meet theirs. This reassures them that you are actually paying attention.

SKILL #3—USE THE TINY, SERENE SMILE.

Provide the most helpful facial expression—the tiny, serene smile. (You don't have to freeze it on your face, of course.) The tiny smile will help you avoid inadvertently frowning or looking sympathetic or worried. Those expressions will distract your partner. The shared expectation of the small smile eliminates any distress over its being, at times, quite artificial.

Few of us are accustomed to being with young people and adults who are discharging emotion. We can become tense, and sometimes, depending on how we were treated when we were young, even alarmed or frightened. We increase our ability to remain aware, relaxed, and warmly attentive no matter what is happening the more we, ourselves, discharge our own emotions.

Definitely, do not look sympathetic. Your partner will notice your response and feel compelled to make you feel comfortable, or less distressed, by withholding discharge.

SKILL #4—REVIEW THE SKILLS TOGETHER

It is your partner's job, and opportunity, to employ the emotional discharge skills. If he/she seems stuck, read the list of skills out loud or ask him/her to read the list of skills to you and share first thoughts for each skill. Even take turns reading the list of discharge skills. Often, one of the skills will suddenly appeal.

In general, though, be ready for eye contact, maintain your small serene smile, don't look worried or sympathetic, and say nothing.

SKILL #5—THE QUESTION: WHAT ARE YOU THINKING?

Ask the question only once, when your partner has stopped talking for three of your inhalations or when he/she has completely stopped discharging emotion. Always, sound interested and relaxed when you ask the question. This is not an interrogation, and you are not looking for information. You are simply encouraging them to share what they are thinking as their thoughts may lead them to discharge.

I hate to plague you with repetition but I must since Life is so important. Right now let's think about the fact that in our everyday interactions with family and friends we often ask, "What have you been doing lately?" We seldom ask, "What have you been thinking about lately?" Yet we are thinking all the time; we think more than we *do*. Won't you make an effort to accustom those you love and care about to the question, "What have you been thinking about lately?" Or, "What are you thinking right now," if the circumstances promise a relaxed, appreciative, or at least interested response rather than confusion, possibly annoyance, and this replay, "What on earth do you mean?"

One of the pleasures of life is sharing with one another our thoughts, ideas, memories, passions, goals, etc., etc. In any situation where at least one other person is present we can volunteer what we have been thinking about lately and then invite others to do the same. Don't confine yourself to family members, either—too limiting. I *do* strangers in store check-out lines.

It's lots of fun!

CHAPTER 42

COMFORTING OTHERS AND EXTENDING OUR COMFORT ZONES

First, let me say this: we were born to comfort one another.   We are a flock animal, or if you prefer, herd, or both flock and herd, or pack or pod or...a vast supercolony or...whatever, we are social animals/beings/spirits and we have a natural desire as well as need to comfort one another and to receive comforting, so when another person is under stress we want to comfort them in a way that truly brings some relief which means to — NOT comfort them.

You know how we do this.   Give the person in your presence the gift of your friendly and primarily silent attention.   If their tears seem close to the surface, tell them in a soft voice, "I believe in crying.   It's okay." You may need to say, "It's okay to cry," several times as they continue to talk with occasional grimaces and tearing. Only IF they obviously are unable to discharge emotion offer a hug or pat or words of comfort, whatever seems sensible to you.

This recommendation to avoid comforting is nothing new, right; the challenge is to resist your conditioning.

You will now encounter some repetition as we think together about *comforting*.

164

Resist. Resist. Resist.

We all have to expand our comfort zone for one another's emotionality (watch for moments when you feel uncomfortable with your own and others' emotionality). We do not want to deliver, with our facial expressions and body movements, the message, "Tamp it down. Go Easy."

Rather, we want our facial expressions to deliver this message: "Go for it! Nothing will upset me!" We need emotional sparks to fly because they can then *burn in* those neural pathways that produce genuine intellectual, emotional, and spiritual liberation. Whenever tears flow freely, **THAT IS THE BRAIN RETRAINING, or as some describe it, REWIRING, itself**.

We all tend to be compulsively comforting even though our comforting efforts only serve to reinforce another person's emotion-avoidance inclinations. Can you remember that? Of course. Can I remember? Sorry, not always. If I am *out in the world* with someone who practices emotional discharge and they become obviously upset, I can still thoughtlessly reach out to pat or hug them. One discharge friend doesn't want <u>any</u> comforting and says, usually, **"Don't."** **This person can sound angry, understandably. I should practice what I** *preach*.

165

Let's imagine: you are sitting at a table and someone you have just met, who sits opposite you, begins to tear up. You instantly recognize the presence of emotion. You think,

"I ought to look away. They must be embarrassed. I'll give them privacy."

But then you say to yourself, "Crying busts stress. They're stressed. I have to help. I must give eye contact so they know it's okay to show how they feel."

So you look at them directly and say in a soft voice something like, "Don't be embarrassed. You need to feel that. It's okay. I believe in crying. It busts stress."

Even if your acquaintance in embarrassment or shame jumps to his/her feet and flees, you have been kind. You have shown them that their emotions deserve to be taken seriously. Through your actions and words you have provided potentially life-changing information.

One more thing! If you start to tear up in public and a thoughtful person says to you that it's okay to cry, why not reply, "You are kind, I believe in crying, it busts stress, I will cry." And cry! Your humiliation-free modeling of this most natural process just may save a life some day and I don't mean yours.

CHAPTER 43

THE UNBELIEVABLY SIGNIFICANT DIFFERENCE BETWEEN FEELING FEELINGS AND EXPERIENCING EMOTIONS

Because our objective is the discharge of emotion, we have to understand the difference between *feeling feelings* and *experiencing emotion*. The difference between feeling feelings and experiencing emotion is critical. It is critical because our culture encourages us to assume that when we feel our feelings we are doing enough; when we talk about our feelings we are doing enough. In certain cases and at certain times that is true. In most cases, and most of the time, if we are under stress, that is **FAR** from the truth.

Here is the difference between feeling feelings and experiencing emotions, in a nutshell.

1. when feeling feelings we are able talk about the *feelings that we feel* and our thoughts, ideas, memories, and images—whatever arises. <u>There are no tears.</u>
2. when experiencing emotion we cry/laugh with tears, normally can't easily talk, and have thoughts, ideas, memories, and images, all being the sources

167

of insight and wisdom, flowing into our conscious and aware minds.

It is not the purpose of this book to address the complex psychological and neurological aspects of the difference between feeling feelings and experiencing emotion. (Semantic differences are rather complex, too.)   We will let neuroscientists and linguists figure all that out and explain it.

Speaking about neuroscientists, I urge them to learn how to experience their emotions through emotional discharge. Then, they will *truly* know the difference between feeling feelings and experiencing emotion...and they might become inspired to begin researching the process.

I need to remind us—or make one additional point—that experts at experiencing emotion are able to abruptly suspend discharge, unhurriedly explain/describe/report what they are thinking (provide listeners with information), and then skillfully plunge back into the state of mind that allows for continued emotional discharge. They are the pros, and we all can become pros also because our marvelous brains are designed to do that.

What happens during those interludes?   Usually they:
1. talk about feelings and thoughts, ideas, images, memories, etc.);

2. connect the dots of cause-and-effect for experiences and relationships; and,
3. draw tentative conclusions about all kinds of things.

CHAPTER 44

ARE TALKING AND *VENTING* EVER A FORM OF EMOTIONAL DISCHARGE?

First, let's define *venting* for those who may be unfamiliar with the term. Venting can mean simply talking as in verbalizing how we feel and what we think; however, you and I are mainly interested in these particular definitions: *giving uninhibited expression to strong emotion, pouring out, verbalizing with energy and force.* (Growing up I never vented! I didn't have strong feelings about anything.)

So, how do we answer the question posed in this chapter's title? This way—talking and venting are <u>never</u> forms of emotional discharge. I address this topic because there is a common belief that some talk and venting can be forms of emotional discharge. Well, although talking and venting can relieve tension, neither is ever a *form* of discharge. If we need to <u>really</u> bust stress we must remember that **tears** <u>are</u> the stress-buster. The deepest most thorough total-body stress relief and also alleviation of emotional pain require emotional discharge.

When we are alone and using discharge skills we do want to take our talking and venting seriously because neither is a waste of time, but when we are using attention with others and they are using attention with us we still want to aim for discharge; talking and venting should be considered stairs on the stairway to the activation and experiencing of emotion with tears.

Talking is, of course, extremely important. When we talk we are thinking, and *skillful emotionality* recommends that whether we *practice* alone or with others, we develop the habit of thinking out loud. But talking and venting are never forms of emotional discharge. Do not let anyone persuade you otherwise. Once we stop discharging emotion, when nothing we say or think about evokes a flowing of emotion with tears, then we talk.

NOTE: after writing this chapter, I discovered that at times I can talk about something painful while tears run down my cheeks. (I have seen other people do this.) Some stress/emotional distress relief results, but only because emotional pain is light, not intense.

I don't intend to settle for talking with tears, though, and I hope that you won't as well because when we settle for tearful talking we fail to access the deeper emotions that when discharged will bring greater total body stress/emotional distress relief as well as greater understanding of ourselves.

Please remember, if you are working with a therapist or are using the attention of a fellow practitioner, talking with tears has value but not ultimate value. You <u>know</u> what yields ultimate value. Go for **that!**

Refuse to
Fear
the Tear.

CHAPTER 45

FLUIDITY OF EMOTION—WHEN WE LAUGH THEN CRY AND CRY THEN LAUGH ARE WE RATIONAL OR HYSTERICAL?

Read this carefully: if you alternate laughing and crying, unless you have a medical diagnosis whose symptomology includes this alternation you are NOT *hysterical* and you ARE *rational* although anxiety/fear may make you think that you are hysterical.

1. Fluidity of emotion is the norm not the exception since the unconscious obeys the *Laws of Association*...one thought triggers another, one emotion triggers other emotions, one thought triggers a chain of emotions and thoughts and vice versa...our brains are like incomprehensibly powerful trains that are responsible for an infinite number of passenger cars that radiate outward on an infinite number of railway tracks, and all are moving at lightning speed, figuratively speaking. Lightning travels at 1/3 the speed of light or 220,000,000 miles per hour. (According to one Internet site the speed of neuron communication can reach up to 330 miles per hour, or 147.5/m/s.)

2. Each thought has its own associated emotion(s). One thought can actually have many emotions associated with it; some will generate laughter, some, tears. One emotion may have many thoughts associated with it; some of those thoughts will generate laughter, some, tears.

When we laugh then cry or vice verse it is good. Laughter reduces tension. If we are practicing skillful emotionality with anyone, including a mental health professional, it is helpful to tell them before we begin practice that if we alternate laughter with crying we are getting rid of tension and for us this is natural. This alternation is also useful: the thoughts that arise during this alternation provide us with valuable information.

Read this carefully, too: when we allow free, uninhibited alternation of laughter and crying, we are allowing our brains to respond with precision to each thought that in sequence arises. We are giving ourselves a needed opportunity to thoroughly experience and obtain relief from the discomfort and confusion of mixed emotions (ambivalence). In an emotion-fearful (emotion-averse) society this opportunity hardly ever appears. So, remember, this fluidity is not a sign of "emotional instability." It is the liberated brain operating smoothly.

It is important to remember that alternation is most likely to occur when we are trying to prolong discharge. The reason: if tension arises during discharge because we are feeling stress, for example, emotions are too intense or unwanted memories are likely to emerge, we will laugh. That laughter reduces tension.   Then, we have the opportunity to pursue discharge at deeper levels or terminate the process by thinking about something that does not evoke emotion.

CHAPTER 46

ADVANCED PRACTICE MEANS INTENTIONALLY PROLONGING DISCHARGE—GOOD OR BAD?

In time, most of us accept the fact that stress-busting and insight benefits increase when we prolong the discharge of emotion. Up until the moment when we recognize this to be true, we often stop our discharge too soon—we notice that we could continue crying or we could stop crying and we think, "Well, probably that was enough."

If we have leaked out a few tears but are still stressed, are still anxious or depressed or uncomfortably energetic and emotionally intense, we might conclude that the process simply doesn't work all the time (or for us, at all). However, lack of relief is simply evidence that we need further discharge.

We always have two choices: re-activate emotion or for the time being accept discomfort. If we choose to accept discomfort that is fine as long as we don't berate ourselves for doing so. It can be wise to accept the discomfort and move on, especially if our tolerance for emotion is still in the early stage of development.

Once we become comfortable with our own emotionality we are able to wisely decide whether or not to prolong discharge and accept greater emotional intensity. The major <u>disadvantage</u> to *intentionally* prolonging emotion is probably obvious. Unless we are deep-emotion tolerant we can find ourselves overwhelmed either by our emotions or by the memories that might surface. Typically, our brains don't take us where we are unprepared to go, but it happens, especially when we are in the company of at least one person who is giving us really focused, relaxed, and caring attention.

Fortunately, we do get clues that we are getting in too close and too deep:

- we suddenly think, "I better stop."
- anxiety or fear arises or we suspect it will, if we don't stop.
- we feel strange or weird, everything around us looks changed even ominous, we feel like a different person...all due to anxiety that we may not consciously detect.
- we suddenly feel intolerably depressed.
- our minds suddenly go blank and all our emotions vanish.
- our eyes keep closing even though we feel awake and/or we feel sleepy, drugged, or numb.
- on the visual screen of our mind we unexpectedly see what I call an artist's canvas

177

where there is no recognizable shape, only blurry colors.

Probably I have forgotten some of the clues.

CHAPTER 47

SUMMARY OF MY OWN ADVANCED PRACTICE EMOTIONAL DISCHARGE

As I have said, I have been practicing skillful emotionality alone and with others for forty-three years and I love doing it. I wish that I could tell you how many hours of actual discharge I have accumulated. If I were like a Tibetan llama I probably could tell you with total confidence the number of hours I have practiced and also the number of hours I have actually discharged emotion during practice.

To amuse myself I just did a calculation by estimating that I have practiced a minimum of two hours a week for forty-three years. You calculate the result if you are bored. Please remember, that is the minimum. (I am not a Tibetan Llama, incidentally. Many llamas can with confidence calculate their meditation hours, and many have accumulated 10,000 hours of meditation, at least.)

Anyway, I want to tell you about my experiences with prolonging emotional discharge. Surprise! I haven't_ had any such experiences To this date (October 2017) I have pretty much accepted *the discharge cycle* (see next chapter) because it has worked. However, by the time you read this book that claim may no longer stand.

You see, the time may soon come when I shall intentionally prolong discharge because I have long had the feeling that I once had an experience that absolutely terrified me.   This does not mean that I was terribly abused, even abused at all.   No.   It means, at the very least, that whatever happened to me I did not understand.

Why do I think that a terrifying experience has yet to surface in consciousness?   In the past, while exchanging time with a partner or partners, the following has occurred:

1. While discharging emotion <u>with my eyes shut</u> I suddenly *sense* that very powerful emotions exist.
2. I sense that terror is one of them.
3. When these conscious concerns arise I often then see in my mind's eye, occupying the entire visual field or canvas of my mind, what looks like an unfinished painting.   The colors are merged and blurred so that nothing is recognizable but I know that my brain has retrieved the scene of a time of terror.
4. When I see it I automatically think, "I don't want to go there."   I open my eyes, cancelling the state of mind that has allowed the scene to emerge.

What now encourages me to decide to prolong discharge? Two recent discharge experiences.

Recently, while crying hard with my eyes shut, I saw what I call an *artist's canvas* in my visual field that resembled a very long tableau. My very first thought was, "Oh no, a timeline." Then I thought, "Oh, no, I don't want to go there." To cancel the brain state that had produced the canvas I opened my eyes and then described the blurry tableau to my partners, John and Wes. I added, "I guess I will have to see what happened sometime soon. My brain obviously needs me to do that. But not now!"

Weeks later, while discharging emotion I again saw the *artist's canvas*, but this time the entire visual field resembled a black and white checkerboard. I have never seen anything like that. Opening my eyes, I described the checkerboard to John and Wes and said, "If I pretend each square is a concrete block than I will imagine myself gradually pulling each block out so that I can see what is behind all of them." Just saying that made me nervous and I again told them that I did not want to *go there*. But I think I will, perhaps soon.

Now why would I want to *dredge* something up that might be <u>really</u> upsetting? For three reasons: to bust stress, to further eliminate sources of potential restimulation, and to achieve what I have named *the transparent brain* which is a brain that harbors no secrets..

181

CHAPTER 48

WHAT IS THE DISCHARGE CYCLE??

You have been crying with awesome success. Two pockets bulge with used tissues. Suddenly, the crying stops. Completely! You think, "What??" You *test out* a few thoughts and re-visualize the image that ought to activate emotion. Nothing. You feel relaxed, but you are upset nevertheless. You had intended to truly *follow your brain* (thoughts/emotions, etc., that arise) and go where you never have been. One specific image which had emerged in a previous exchange of attention was definitely going to ferry you somewhere new, but where'd all the emotion go? Where, where, where??

Well, when no more emotion seems available for a specific thought, image, or memory, etc., you can conclude that for the moment, for a number of logical reasons, you have completed a discharge cycle for that particular thought or memory, etc. The absence of emotion does not indicate that there is no more emotion associated with whatever was on your mind. No. In fact, if you are determined, you can experiment with each skill just in case one of the skills activates dischargeable emotion, but it's fine to accept the cessation of emotionality and discharge.

Why is it fine for us to accept the cessation? Because our efforts are not wasted even when we don't *go as far* as we

182

had hoped to go.   You see, our brains have stored all the details of our inner journey up to the point when discharge stopped.   So, when we recollect and re-imagine the details of the discharge experience we will, if we are able to provide our brains with enough <u>repetition</u>, re-activate emotion and *journey on*!   And what do I mean by *repetition*?   At a relaxed pace, repeat aloud words/thoughts, re-describe experiences, re-visualize all the images the arose during the experience, and using skills proceed with new content that arises.

Now how do I know that you can pick up where you left off?   Guess.

I often write down the thoughts, etc., that were arising just before discharge ceased.   You might want to do that, too.

CHAPTER 49

HOW I LEARNED ABOUT THE PRACTICE OF EMOTIONAL DISCHARGE

I think that it's time that I tell you about my initial experience with emotional discharge practice and with the educational, peer counseling program that, thank goodness for me, introduced it to me. (I know that learning to discharge emotion saved my life. I know that being unable to discharge emotion nearly ended it.)

Nearly five years after my discharge from the hospital, April 1974, I was overstressed and high. Not that anyone knew this. To others I would have appeared to be full of energy and creative ideas. I was overstressed because that January I had assumed my first truly responsible job, that of administrative assistant to the Executive Director of the Mental Health Association of Connecticut. So ironic, I think.

Within that first month of working I began heading for trouble, the kind of trouble that we all want to avoid: lots of restimulated thinking, ideas, memories, and desires. I was not aware of being scared, of course, because I was high.

The wonderful man who hired me, John Abbot, a former minister of a Congregational Church, United Church of Christ (UCC), my Protestant denomination at that time,

184

knew of my psychiatric hospitalization because I had promptly told him about it when he interviewed me. So I felt that he was taking a risk with me. Consciously, and not only for my own sake, I feared failing.

So, lucky me, April 1974, a friend invited me to attend this ongoing educational class that she was investigating. It was offered by a teacher of something called Re-evaluation Counseling. My friend had already attended eight classes and she thought I might find the program interesting. (I think that she suspected that I was having problems.)

So, there I was in a stranger's home with about ten other people including my friend, seated in a spacious living room. The teacher, a young woman named Joette, explained why the emotional discharge process is so useful and told us that in our classes we would be encouraged to eliminate any barriers to using this process. At the time I did not realize that she was really saying, "You are going to deprogram yourself and retrain your brain." (If she had said that I might have jumped up and fled.)

She explained why this peer counseling program utilized the equal-time format and of course it made sense to me—whatever our age, everyone needs warm, patient, focused attention for thinking and dealing with emotions, and hardly anyone receives it. Practically everyone is so eager to talk about their own ideas and experiences that they interrupt one another or at least hardly hear one another.

With the equal-time format even the most quiet person receives attention. No participant can dominate the class and quiet people have time to think and experience emotion without interruption. (I had no idea that this equal-time format would prove to be the life-saving feature that it was, for me.)

What an experience that first class was!! For the first time in my life I watched several people weep with little to no embarrassment. It was an eye opener, especially when I watched a young man sob over failing to do a good job at something. He was feeling like a failure and he appeared to be heartbroken.

At the end of that first class a stranger (I learned later that her name was Rachel) offered me a hug. Reluctantly, I accepted and was horrified when I immediately exploded in hot messy tears. Rachel continued to hug me, reminding me that tears were something to celebrate and I shouldn't worry if I didn't know why I was crying.

Then, I certainly didn't know why I cried but I did know how I felt after that burst of intense emotion and tears—great! I felt great! So, feeling impossibly energized I announced at the end of this class that I would join the it for the next seven sessions. I left her home exhilarated and elated.

Now, normally, we who swing high might be wary of any activity that could so quickly produce an effect like this one. Fortunately, my lack of concern was justified for one reason: I left the class absent tons of stress. Because of that flood of tears, I not only busted stress that I unconsciously had been feeling at my new and quite challenging job, but my brain (or my subconscious or whatever) *knew* I now had a reliable outlet for tension and stress. Believe me, I did not recognize that.

And why did I explode with emotion? *Restimulation*, of course. The young man's suffering and tears had provided me with just the right trigger for my own *restimulation* and stress-busting discharge. What was the trigger? His feeling of being a failure, of course. As you may remember, two days before I attempted suicide (September, 1968) I had quit my teaching job. I had felt that I was a failure, a perfect failure, in fact. (I wasn't, and neither are you!!!)

CHAPTER 50

THE <u>VERY</u> PRIMAL SCREAM

While reviewing the previous chapter I recalled something that I had remembered earlier but forgotten to talk about. This is it: in a sense, <u>I was actually prepped (prepared) for a program that focused on crying.</u>

What prepared me for emotional discharge? I had just finished reading a book that I highly recommend, **THE PRIMAL SCREAM, The Cure for Neurosis** by psychologist Arthur Janov, a clinical psychologist, first published in 1970.

While I was reading this book, which describes Dr. Janov's work with patients, I burst into hot and heavy tears. I doubt that I understood why that happened, but since I cried in response to something I was reading rather than to an actual present time experience I felt no alarm. Dr. Janov's patients screamed and cried and received respect, not criticism. They were applauded, not condemned. Their response was desirable, was good. They were considered normal so I and my tears had to be normal, too. Thanks to Janov I learned my tears were natural. This is exactly what I hope you will discover, too.

Weeks later, when I burst into tears at that Re-evaluation Counseling gathering, I no longer associated tears with falling apart or with being *weak*. (Can you believe the timing? Was I lucky or what to find Janov's book!)

Incidentally, I had no idea Janov died October of the year I am writing this book, 2017. I am so sorry that I never contacted him to let him know that his book prepared me to eagerly embrace the life-saving life-changing opportunity of Re-evaluation Counseling.

Because his book made such an impression on me I want to talk a little more about Janov. He believed that practically all of our mental health as well as many of our physical health problems resulted from unhealed traumatic experiences of early infancy/childhood. He designed a therapeutic approach that enabled his patients to relive specific traumatic events. During reliving there usually was one moment of enormously intense emotion when the patient would spontaneously let out a heart rending scream of psychological pain and understanding (insight).

CHAPTER 51

RE-EVALUATION COUNSELING AND PRIMAL THERAPY

I forgot to tell you that Re-evaluation Counseling as a practice was founded in the early 1950's by my hero, Carl Harvey Jackins, a nonprofessional who discovered, while helping the enormously distressed friend of a friend, that paying warm patient attention to a person and allowing them to be uninhibitedly emotional could have extremely positive results—like recovery. That person's experience persuaded Harvey to experiment with curious friends; the best way to do it proved to be to trade time, to give one another equal time. Ring a bell?

Harvey published his first book of theory, **THE HUMAN SIDE OF HUMAN BEINGS,** in 1968. This book explains in lay terms why emotional discharge is one of our most valuable natural physiological processes.

Over the years, Re-evaluation Counseling evolved into the educational peer counseling community that it is today. Its sole purpose is to help people help one another recover their ability to use the discharge process. The Re-evaluation Counseling Communities, Inc., provides participants with a worldwide community of practitioners. Participation can be lifelong for those who find it rewarding. I have practiced discharge for more than half my life but most of the time I have not been a member of the community.   Location, obligation, and scheduling problems prevented that.

If you read Janov's book you will see that both he and Jackins developed programs that focus on helping us activate the *emotional discharge process*.   There are differences between the programs and the theories that support them, of course, and as both programs are still in operation there still are differences.   One major difference: Janov's program is provided by professionals trained in his therapeutic approach while Re-evaluation Counseling is peer taught with all trained teachers not only providing theory, etc., but, like everyone else in the class, assuming each role, that of counselor and of client.

Think about purchasing Janov and Jackins' books.   If you find skillful emotionality helpful you will find their books helpful, also.

Janov's book has something very special to offer, descriptions of the therapeutic experiences of humans just like us!!!   While reading about someone's breakthrough you may cry, as I did,.   You might like to prime your brain for tears; set a box of tissues or roll of toilet paper beside you whenever you read his book.

Jackin's book has something very special to offer as well, a theory of human nature, behavior, and potential that is based on people's actual experiences with exchanging

attention and with discharge.   I found his book
enlightening and inspirational.

CHAPTER 52

LET'S THINK ABOUT GETTING THE RIGHT KIND OF HELP #2

Working with mental health professionals is serious business.   You do not want to waste your time or your money...or your life.   Many professionals do not know how to be helpful and self-harm and suicide, or homicide, can result and has resulted.

Professionals, on the whole, will not have encountered many clients who to some degree want to be in charge of their sessions and, among other things, specifically want silent attention for the discharge of emotion.   Fortunately, enlisting their support for this is not difficult as long as you explain that busting stress is one of your objectives and you know that crying does this, for you.   Probably, you will need, also, to reassure them that you don't intend to spend the entire session working on the discharge of emotion.   Most therapists do have valuable knowledge to share and they are eager to share it.

The professional most likely will have done little crying her or himself and will only intellectually understand its value.   Rare is the professional who practices emotional discharge although such individuals do exist; many teach Re-evaluation Counseling.   Your objective will be to make yourself feel safe discharging emotion with someone who may believe that your time could be better spent discussing your situation, etc.. If you set things up for yourself at every session that will help.

At the beginning of each session let her/him know that (1) you need to *cry a little* without interruption so that you can get rid of tension and (2) it would help if at each session a block of time were set aside for that. Explain that you stay focused more easily if they don't say anything until you report that you are ready for them to do so and that comments, observations, questions, and advice, though useful, will make it harder for you to notice feelings and emotion.

Of course, you might prefer not to *set things up* each session. In that case, here are two things I have said to professionals just before discharge began:

> "Do you mind if I cry right now?"
> "I've got to cry for a bit."

Let them know that you might laugh, too, *because it reduces tension.* If you suspect that you might laugh while describing some horrendous thoughts or incidents, tell them this, also. Often, when I am recalling a painful incident, especially one that originally evoked feelings of horror, remorse, or rage, I begin discharge with laughter. That is totally normal!

Laughter reduces tension, even tension of which we are unaware.

CHAPTER 53

MEDITATION AND SKILLFUL EMOTIONALITY—BOY DO THEY COMPLEMENT ONE ANOTHER!

We want to take a look at the similarity between meditation and skillful emotionality. Because I meditate at least once a week thanks to the wonderful *sangha* (practice community) at my Unitarian Universalist Congregation, I am familiar with meditation and I find the similarity intriguing. Obviously, the practice of *skillful emotionality* is not exactly like meditation...in fact, the two practices seem to be totally in opposition to one another. However, both practices have a great deal in common and offer numerous benefits to those of us who are vulnerable to depression/mood swings.

Incidentally, I consider what is called *mindfulness meditation* to be so extremely useful for anyone who wants to learn to reduce stress that I recommend the proven stress-reduction program described in the book, **FULL CATASTROPHE LIVING: Using the Wisdom of Your Body & Mind to Face Stress, Pain & Illness,** by Jon Kabat-Zinn. The program that Kabat-Zinn created in 1979, and that he and colleagues refined over the years, is named Mindfulness Based Stress Reduction (MBSR). Impressive, it incorporates mindfulness meditation, body awareness, yoga, and in most cases, counseling.   Programs are offered in a wide variety of venues.

Now, please don't imagine that I am suggesting that you eventually replace the practice of skillful emotionality with any form of meditation or with MBSR.   **Oh, no, no.**   Meditation and skillful emotionality complement one another.   Meditation helps us generate a quiet, peaceful, yet aware and often thought-full mind with relaxed body.   Skillful emotionality helps us generate an, aware, thought-full, and highly stimulated yet relaxed mind with energized body.

Both meditation and skillful emotionality reconnect us with our bodies, thoughts, ideas, memories, feelings, and emotions.   With both, images can appear in our mind's eye.   With both we can suddenly relive experiences. Practice outcomes are also similar: reduced stress; increased self-awareness, insight, wisdom, and empathy for all living beings; greater patience and less impulsivity; and feelings of gratitude for precious life.   Both practices tend to help us feel more connected with one another and with all aspects of Life and Reality, producing, therefore, sentiments and feelings that I label *spiritual*.   (The list of benefits is much longer than what I provide here.)

Both practices have so much to offer.   In our highly distracting technological society re-connection with others, with our needs and desires, and especially with our deepest selves and one another's preciousness, is essential. A refreshed state of mind permits us to more thoroughly enjoy all of our relationships. Greater awareness enables us to really be present with one another, giving and receiving attention, love, affection, and emotional support. Yes, each practice has so much to offer. You deserve both. I do, too! At a recent meeting of our sangha I had a meditation experience that actually felt sweet; my entire body and mind achieved absolute peace. I will never forget that experience. I will not <u>try</u> to achieve it again, however. As per meditation instructions we are not supposed to try to attain any particular mental/physical state. Now, here is something that I find fascinating. Successful meditation seems to require that we do the opposite of what we do to successfully discharge emotion.

Meditation   Emotional Discharge

Meditation	Emotional Discharge
Notice/observe <u>feelings and emotions</u>, even label or name them (i.e., *sadness*), but **do not linger** with them and instead return to the object of your attention (could be a mantra, a visual image, a sound, etc.).	Notice <u>feelings and emotions</u>, **linger** with them, focus attention on them, and use skills to elicit discharge. Label or name feelings/emotions if discharge might be activated by doing so.
Notice/observe all <u>thoughts</u>, even say "thinking" or "thought," or use other technique, but **do not linger** with them.	Notice/observe all <u>thoughts</u> and **linger** with them, using discharge skills if any seem to evoke a physical or emotional response.

If you are unfamiliar with meditation you may be surprised, also, at some of the assumptions that both practices make regarding our species. Because there are many meditation traditions, and because I am not well informed about any of them, really, what I write here may not hold true for all of the traditions. Nevertheless, I want you to know that here are two what appear to be extremely contradictory ideas that interest me somewhat and that you should be prepared for. I hope that you won't worry about them. We who do emotional discharge don't really focus on these ideas at all. Notice if distress arises when you read them!!! That's a clue that at some point tension/distress has been triggered and discharge would be helpful.

Meditation	Emotional Discharge
We are not our feelings and emotions, which are constantly changing.	We are our feelings and emotions, which are constantly changing.
We are not our thoughts, which are constantly changing.	We have thoughts and they can be constantly changing.
During meditation, no thought is so important that we must cling to it, focus attention on it.	During emotional discharge practice every thought deserves our conscious attention; none should be ignored or discounted.

I must add, I really am astounded by the fact that with skillful emotionality I can bust a ton of felt stress in thirty seconds or less.   I do, therefore, encourage meditators to become adept at practicing skillful emotionality.

Would I ever suggest omitting meditation from a stress-busting, insight-generating toolkit?   No!   I encourage anyone who practices emotional discharge to learn to meditate if the desire to do so arises.   Each practice produces results that are essential to our wellbeing.

I do not suggest that these two practices be combined, however.   No, no, no!   Each should be practiced separately so that expertise in each is achieved and maintained.

CHAPTER 54

MEDITATION, EMOTIONAL DISCHARGE, AND *THE UNEXPECTED*

Remember my warning regarding emotional discharge?   Here it is.   Please reread it.   It applies to meditation, also.   Below you will learn why I say this.

WARNING

<u>BE ADVISED</u>: EMOTIONAL DISCHARGE <u>CAN</u> UNEXPECTEDLY *UNLOCK* THOUGHTS/IDEAS, FEELINGS, EMOTIONS, AND MEMORIES THAT WE ARE NOT READY TO NOTICE (OR EXPERIENCE) AND CONSCIOUSLY THINK ABOUT.   SOMETIMES IT IS WISE TO CRY IN THE PRESENCE OF A SKILLED AND TRUSTED THERAPIST WHO HAS ALREADY STATED HIS OR HER CONFIDENCE THAT CRYING HAS VALUE.

Because I highly recommend meditation to anyone who wants to bust stress, I need to share information from an article that I encountered online which lists unexpected and unwanted experiences that one can have during and after meditation.   I believe that those of us who practice emotional discharge can experience some of them.

Now, the online article.   It was provided by *Quartz* on May 29, 2017: "There's A Dark Side to Meditation That No One Talks About," by Lila MacLellan.

200

According to MacLellan, two experienced meditators, Jared Lindahl, a professor of religious studies, and Willoughby Britton, a psychologist and assistant professor of psychiatry, interviewed 60 Western Buddhist meditation practitioners who had experienced what I will call *the unexpected* during practice. Newcomers to meditation as well as teachers were interviewed. All interviewed were practicing one of the following meditation traditions: Theravada, Zen, or Tibetan. Some meditators had accumulated more than 10,000 hours of practice.

Unexpected experiences, which the authors called *challenging issues*, included: anxiety and fear, nausea, insomnia, irritability, re-experiencing past trauma, **a sense of total detachment from emotion, time and space, perception problems, hallucinations, and hypersensitivity to light or sound.**.

I don't believe that emotional dischargers ordinarily have the bolded experiences. If during emotional discharge or meditation you do have one or more unexpected and undesirable experience <u>and</u> distress persists, you will want to let someone know. Meditation teachers and psychotherapists are ready to help.

201

CHAPTER 55

THE BRILLIANT BRAIN AT WORK—TWO ADVENTURES!

I have concluded that many of us decide to check out the practice of meditation because we have read, *meditation will allow you to truly experience your natural mind*, a statement that is true, in my opinion. If that is an enticement for you then this might make you happy—during the emotional discharge process we get to experience the natural mind and how the brain *brings to our aware attention information that it has stored.* (Remember, to the brain, <u>everything</u> that happens in mind and body is information.)

Here is what I mean about experiencing the brain at work—twice now, while discharging, I have spied in the upper right hand corner of my inner visual field (eyes closed during discharge) a rectangle with a border. We know that borders attract attention. Right? Newspapers and Internet websites use them all the time to help us focus our attention. Our brain uses them when we discharge, too. And they certainly attract attention. Here are two *rectangle experiences* which I found to be awesome.

1. During the first experience, in the 80's, I was discharging emotion with the most skillful therapist I ever had, Robert P. Belliveau, LCSW. Suddenly, while I discharged, a rectangle with a dark interior

and light border appeared.   It was a strange painting nailed to the vertical wall of my mind. Knowing exactly how to best focus my attention on the image, I applied the discharge skill of repetition and repeatedly described the image to Bob until the expected-unexpected happened.   The rectangular image abruptly reoriented itself so that I hovered above it and was staring down at it.   The rectangle then morphed into a circle and began to rotate counterclockwise.   Brilliant colors that appeared out of nowhere were flung outward as though the rectangle had become a centrifuge, and the colors accumulated on the walls of the circle until, to my astonishment, I found myself looking down at my kitchen at home: the dark interior of the rectangle was the wood kitchen table and the light border was the linoleum floor.   Instantly, I remembered: while I was a senior in college at home on vacation, my kind dad asked me how I would feel if he divorced my mom.   I totally freaked out; he chased me around the table, possibly in a counterclockwise direction, in a loving effort to hold and comfort me. I think I fled to the basement.   Afterwards, I said no word to anyone in my family and that afternoon took a bus to my college dorm an hour away.   By then I had locked this emotion-packed memory in a box and buried it.   Now, it was out of the box.

This time I cried buckets and discovered that the idea of a divorce had terrified me and I would have fallen apart and never graduated had my parents divorced because I had no emotional resilience whatsoever. I still thank my dad for his honesty and his sacrifice. I thank my brain, too.

2. During the second experience, probably in 2005, while discharging I spied a rectangle that had suddenly appeared. Deciding that I was looking at an open window I *zoomed* closer and peered out...at endless blackness plus myriad white dots. Stars? I seemed to be looking into deep space, into infinity, in fact. Unfortunately, when I described what I saw a well-meaning person with whom I was practicing commented on my verbal description and as a result I had an instant interpretation that although extremely exciting to contemplate had to immediately be discounted due to the influence of the remark because my thinking had been *contaminated*. Although I didn't criticize my partner I was extremely disappointed. I wondered if useful information would have been *delivered* had she said nothing

Yes, during discharge you will experience how your fascinating brain works. It will work <u>really</u> well because you will not be inhibiting it!

It's funny, but I never would have guessed that the brain naturally uses borders <u>during discharge</u>.   Oh, what brains we have!!

> *I think my brain is feeling a little embarrassed*
> *by all of the praise I have heaped upon it.*
> *Think that's possible?*

You will be heaping praise on your brain, too, and don't let borders or geometric shapes or ANYTHING you see in your mind's eye throw you for a loop, at least if you can help it.   Your brain neurons are conscientiously processing information especially for YOU.   They are like the United States Postal Service.   *Neither snow nor rain nor heat nor gloom of night stays these* (neurological) *couriers from the swift completion of their appointed rounds* (of information retrieval).

CHAPTER 56

EMOTIONAL DISCHARGE VERSUS MIND-ALTERING SUBSTANCES—THE WINNER IS?

Until scientific research proves me wrong, I proclaim emotional discharge the winner. We who deal with our vulnerability take note, please.

For a wide variety of reasons some of us experiment with mind-altering substances. I am not going to list the reasons. For a wide variety of reasons I never did. I am not going to list those reasons.

I will say this—I _am_ grateful that I never tried any mind-altering substances other than caffeine because if I had, perhaps I would not have been motivated to learn to bust stress, prevent depression, and eliminate harmful mood swings using a free, easy to access, natural process—emotional discharge. (Who knows?)

I am not saying that no mind-altering substance has value. Definitely not. I believe that mind-altering substances possess more value than we can imagine and we are lucky that some universities and colleges and other institutions are researching their potential. Eventually, they may prove far more useful than some, or most, pharmaceutical products/medications.

So why this bias against mind-altering substances? I may be wrong, but I don't <u>think</u> any mind-altering substance reliably busts stress, improving the condition and functioning of the entire body (physically, not just mentally). Regular use of mind-altering substances may relieve tension for hours or days or weeks or months or years, but the rewards <u>might</u> always be limited, not comprehensive. For example, they may (1) prolong the need/desire for continued us, (2) deprive the individual of some of the benefits listed in Chapters 9 and 10, and (3) possibly cause brain damage.

Now those are assumptions, only. I am not talking at all about the psychotherapeutic effects of mind-altering substances, which exist.

A dear friend, Chris, has pointed this out to me: "Pam, you never stop needing to discharge emotion. You say you ought to do it at least once a week, if you are smart. So how can it be working?" I didn't think to tell him this: I am vulnerable to stress-induced depression/mood swings, that is why.

Young people who are vulnerable to depression/mood swings deserve to achieve emotional discharge proficiency, which means they can discharge emotion when, where, with whom, and to what intensity, they choose. Please, if you are a young person, learn to enjoy your brain on YOU using emotional discharge. Organize exchanges with family members/friends so that you and everyone else receives warm, patient, silent attention for sharing and experiencing emotion.

Looking for adventure? Excitement? Suspense? Our species' free, easy to access, natural, stress busting, information retrieving, awareness heightening, consciousness extending, empathy and compassion expanding, insight liberating, and confidence building process just might astonish you.

Your terrific brain may give you a terrific ride as well as prove to be your personal terminator of depression and "harmful" mood swings.

PART FOUR

THE PROCESS: SECTION TWO

Repetition may save your life!

Any repetition of ideas in the following pages is

just for you!

♥

CHAPTER 57

LET *EMOTIONAL LIBERATION* BEGIN RIGHT NOW FOR ALL OUR CHILDREN AND YOUNG PEOPLE

Whether or not they have inherited a vulnerability to depression and mood swings, all our children and young people are damaged by the social programming that we address here in this book. It usually doesn't look as though they are damaged, does it, but this is the truth: they <u>all</u> are. Trust me. Without the freedom to discharge emotion they have no way to easily and naturally reduce stress, and worse, they cannot be their true selves when they are in the company of family, friends, and others in their lives. If they cannot be themselves, be how they actually feel, they become distanced from themselves as well as from those they love and who love them. They are forced to endure or repress the pain of loneliness, separation, and isolation. **There are decisions, simple and harmless and simple and harmful, that they would never make if they were free to discharge emotion at the *right* time, the *right* place, to the *right* intensity, and with the *right* people.**

In my past (1950's and 1960's) adults and professionals acknowledged that the pre-teen and teen years could be years of terrible emotional turmoil for many young people, but there were few if any educational and

210

therapeutic programs for young people and for parents. Parents hoped that the pre-teen and teen years would pass as quickly as possible without disaster...professionals became involved only when young people obviously were falling or had fallen into the quicksand of deep distress.

Now (2017) educational and therapeutic programs have already proliferated. Why? I am not going to list the reasons. However, I will provide you with some un-cited information and statistics of which I had been totally unaware.

1. Anxiety disorders can begin with worrying and nervousness, often by the age of six and seven. About 30% of young people age 18-29 suffer from anxiety and 58% of those who have experienced a major depressive disorder have an anxiety disorder, also.
2. Staff at residential programs that include K-12 education as well as therapy and every other type of healthful activity that you can imagine find, during casual and guided conversations with young people and also through self-reporting and testing, that social media seems to be contributing a great deal to the incidence of anxiety.

So, what do <u>we</u> do? Us? You and me? For one thing, let's no longer say to a child, "I'll give you something to cry about," if he or she begins to shed tears. I mention this right now because I recently learned that someone I referred to earlier in this book, who cannot cry no matter what, heard those words during childhood. Can you imagine the impact? Of course!

By now I hope it is obvious what we need to do. We need to help our children and young people learn how to utilize the emotional discharge process with an expertise that we can only hope to obtain.

We do not want to make life harder for our young people than it needs to be? Therefore, please resolve to begin your own deprogramming right now by allowing children and young people that you encounter to be emotional in your presence no matter how uncomfortable and conflicted you feel. Frankly and directly, tell them it is okay to be emotional; you don't want them to have to pretend they feel good when they don't; you don't want them to have to hold in emotions if they have them; you are beginning to understand that sounding how they feel when they talk makes sense; and you are learning that crying is a wise and helpful thing to do, for them and for you. Tell them!

Tell them! Tell them that they deserve to be proud of themselves when they discharge emotion and you will be proud of them, too, because it is an intelligent thing to do. Hearing your words will help them liberate themselves.

I'm not saying anything that you probably haven't heard. More than anything, children and young people seek our acceptance, warmth, and patient prolonged attention for emotion and talk not just for doing chores together, playing games and sports together, watching TV together, shopping together, etc. *Togetherness* is a good thing...but we must ensure that relaxed exchanges of information and displays of emotion, when emotion is present, become the norm, not the exception.

During the good and easy times we win their trust gradually by listening quietly, warmly, and well when they initiate conversation and by often inviting them to share what they think about and what they are actually thinking at the moment. We have to avoid interrupting them, commenting, interrogating, or compulsively sharing our own similar experiences and our own opinions and beliefs, etc. By doing so we will keep the path to emotionality clear. Below is one way I have tried to keep communication lines open with the young people that I encounter.

I have not been in the company of too many young people in my lifetime. I will never forget the first time that I asked a young person who was around six years old, "What are you thinking?" I really doubted that she would know what I meant. Did she even know what a *thought* was? How ignorant I was! She began sharing her thoughts immediately.

First, I say this, "Do you mind if I share some things that I'm thinking about?" (I share a few things, keeping it brief.)

Then I say, "Would you like to share some things that you're thinking about?"

CHAPTER 58

SINCE *BIG BOYS DON'T CRY* IT TAKES A **REALLY** BIG BOY TO CRY!

I interviewed my emotional discharge partner, John, who began the interview by saying the revealing words you now read in the chapter title above.   Just in case you have no time to read this chapter at this time (or ever) you ought to know this: **one episode of four harsh spankings when he was two years old changed his life and also increased his vulnerability to depression.   That is his opinion, not mine.**

To save myself time I am leaving the text in caps as originally taken by dictation.   Hope this is acceptable to you.   When we self-publish we really can do anything we please.

♥

I asked John to tell me what happened to him.

I WAS TWO YEARS OLD AND I WAS CRYING.   I DON'T KNOW WHY I WAS CRYING.   SOMETHING HAD HAPPENED.   I DON'T KNOW WHAT I WAS CRYING ABOUT.   I GUESS TWO YEAR OLDS ARE NOT EXPECTED TO **NOT** CRY.

MY FATHER HEARD ME AND HE HIT ME ON THE BOTTOM AND SAID, "DRY UP." THIS WAS PAINFUL SO I CRIED LOUDER. AND HE HIT ME ON THE BOTTOM AGAIN AND SAID LOUDER, "DRY UP." SO I CRIED LOUDER. **AND ABOUT THE FOURTH TIME THIS HAPPENED HE HIT ME ON THE BOTTOM VERY HARD AND IT WAS VERY PAINFUL AND IT WAS LIKE SOMETHING BROKE INSIDE ME LIKE STEPPING ON A DRY TWIG IN THE WOODS, AND I STOPPED CRYING AND THAT'S WHAT HE WANTED ME TO DO. WHATEVER BROKE INSIDE I THINK IS STILL BROKEN.**

SOMETHING WAS WRONG HERE AND I KNEW IT. WHEN A KID IS CRYING YOU SHOULD NOT HURT HIM. YOU SHOULD ACTUALLY SHOW SOME SYMPATHY AND LISTEN TO HIM CRY, BUT THAT DIDN'T HAPPEN.

SO I DIDN'T CRY. I QUIT CRYING. BUT WHATEVER IT IS THAT BROKE THAT TIME IS STILL BROKEN. NOW THAT I AM 82 YEARS OLD IT'S STILL BROKEN. AND I DIDN'T REALIZE THAT SOME TRAUMA THAT HAD HAPPENED AT THE AGE OF TWO CHANGED LIFE FOREVER FOR

ME. SO, NO LONGER DID I STAND UP FOR MYSELF. I JUST DIDN'T STAND UP FOR MYSELF A LOT OF TIME IN MY LIFE.

WHEN I WAS ABOUT 12 YEARS OLD I WAS IN THE KITCHEN AND HE WAS SITTING AT THE TABLE AND HE SAID SOMETHING THAT WAS UNKIND. I DON'T REMEMBER WHAT IT WAS AND I BECAME ANGRY AND PICKED UP A COFFEE POT AND THREW IT AT THE WALL ABOVE HIS HEAD. I HADN'T INTENDED TO HURT HIM BECAUSE WHATEVER WAS BROKEN IN ME DIDN'T LIKE ME WANTING TO HURT ANYBODY. THE COFEE POT HIT THE WALL A LOT CLOSER THAN I HAD PLANNED.

THEN THERE WAS A TIME WHEN I WAS 15 OR 16 WHEN HE SAID SOMETHING THAT WAS UNKIND. I BECAME ENRAGED AGAIN AND I THREW THE KITCHUP BOTTLE AT HIM AND IT HIT THE CABINET DOOR BEHIND HIM, STILL ABOVE HIS HEAD. IT BROKE THE CABINET DOOR INTO TWO PIECES. I DON'T KNOW IF I BROKE THE KETCHUP BOTTLE. VERY TOUGH GLASS, APPARENTLY.

♥

(THIS IS VERY IMPORTANT) I asked him if he wanted to talk about the therapist who let him down big time.

YES. WHEN I WAS 17 YEARS OLD I WAS BACK FROM CHICAGO. I HAD BEEN ALLOWED TO SKIP MY SENIOR YEAR AND I HAD BEEN GOING TO COLLEGE THERE.

I HAD A VERY BAD SCHOOL YEAR AND I WAS VERY DEPRESSED. AND MY MOTHER WAS AWARE OF THIS. MY FATHER WAS NEVER AWARE WHEN I WAS FEELING BAD OR FEELING GOOD BUT MY MOTHER WAS AWARE SO SHE TOOK ME TO THE COLLEGE TO THE PSYCHOLOGICAL DEPT AND GOT ME A BATTERY OF TESTS. THE RESULT OF THE TESTS WAS I COULD USE PSYCHOTHERAPY

SO I STARTED WITH AN M.D., NAME OMITTED. I THINK IT WAS IN THE SUMMER. I KNEW THAT I WAS AFRAID TO TALK ABOUT WHAT REALLY BOTHERED ME. I WENT TO HIM EVERY WEEK AND AFTER ABOUT 6 MONTHS OF THIS I FINALLY BUILT UP ENOUGH COURAGE TO START TALKING ABOUT WHAT MY PROBLEM WAS, THAT IS TO DEAL WITH THE SITUATION THAT I'D COME TO THERAPY FOR.

I REMEMBER THE DAY I SHOWED UP IN HIS OFFICE. I WAS EXPERIENCING AN EXTREME AMOUNT OF FEAR BECAUSE I INTENDED TO GO THROUGH IT AND START THE CONVERSATION WHERE IT WAS MEANT TO BE.

WHEN I SHOWED UP IN THE DOCTOR'S OFFICE HE SAID, "<u>YOU REALLY LOOK UPSET. WHATEVER UPSET YOU, DON'T TALK ABOUT IT NOW.</u>"

THAT WAS THE MOMENT OF HIS FAILURE. I NEVER DID TALK ABOUT IT. I SAW HIM A YEAR AND A HALF MORE SO THAT WAS 2 YEARS. I NEVER BROUGHT UP THE SUBJECT AGAIN. WE TALKED ABOUT SMALL ISSUES BUT WE DIDN'T TALK ABOUT THE THING I'D SHOWED UP IN HIS OFFICE TO TALK ABOUT.

♥

I asked if he wanted to share what happened when in 1977 he attended Erhard Seminars Training (EST), now Landmark.

WHEN I WAS THIRTY-FIVE I ENCOUNTERED SOME PEOPLE WHO WERE INTO EST. THE PROGRAM HAS A DIFFERENT NAME, NOW.

SO I WENT TO A COFFEE SEMINAR. I WAS IMPRESSED WITH WHAT THEY HAD TO SAY AND I SIGNED UP TO DO THE TRAINING. GENERALLY A LOT OF PEOPLE CAME TO THOSE EST EVENTS BUT ONLY A SMALL PERCENTAGE SIGNED UP FOR THE PROGRAM SO THEY DID LOTS OF GUEST EVENTS.

THE SUMMER OF 1977 I SHOWED UP FOR THE TRAINING. EST WAS DEFINITELY LIFE CHANGING FOR ME. I GOT THRU MY FEAR OF SHARING WHAT I'D GONE TO THERAPY TO TALK ABOUT.

EST HAD A PROGRAM CALLED *COMMUNICATION WORKSHOP*. AFTER THE FIRST TRAINING I SIGNED UP FOR THIS COMMUNICATION WORKSHOP BECAUSE I KNEW I WANTED TO COMMUNICATE WHAT I'D NEVER COMMUNICATED. AND I WENT THRU FOUR DAYS OF THE COMMUNICATION WORKSHOP AND STILL HADN'T COMMUNICATED SO I SIGNED UP TO REVIEW IT A MONTH LATER.

AFTER TWO DAYS OF THE WORKSHOP, ON DAY 3, I SHARED WHAT WAS GOING ON WITH ME TO A WHOLE ROOM FULL OF PEOPLE. NO ONE EMBARRASSED ME. THEY WERE PROUD THAT I'D BROKEN THROUGH.

I SHARED THAT I'D GONE THRU THIRTY-FIVE
YEARS OF LIFE WITHOUT THIS BREAKTHROUGH,
WITHOUT COMMUNICATING ABOUT IT, AND I
DID COMMUNICATE ABOUT IT THE SECOND
TIME OF THE COMMUNICATION WORKSHOP, ON
DAY THREE.   SINCE THEN I'VE BEEN ABLE TO
TALK ABOUT IT .

♥

**I asked him if he wanted to talk about his belief that
his father's punishment had contributed to his not
finishing things or his not wanting to finish things.
He shared something else, instead.**

WHEN HE FORCED ME TO STOP CRYING AND
SOMETHING BROKE IN THERE MY SENSE OF
FAIRNESS AND RIGHTNESS WAS DESTROYED.
I WAS FORCED INTO BASICALLY A LIE.

I GUESS THAT'S ENOUGH FOR ME NOW.

Was it enough for you, enough to persuade you that your
children need to receive warm patient attention for tears
and sobbing?   Was it enough to convince you that
punishment for tears can lead to long term harm?

CHAPTER 59

CRYBABY

All young people suffer the judgment of others if they discharge emotion in public (and anywhere else, actually, including at home).   However, right now it is necessary to acknowledge that although the programming for all of our children is damaging, our male children and young people are likely to suffer more <u>social condemnation</u> than our female children and young people.   Presently, and tragically, boys and young men who leak even a few tears while in the presence of other boys and young men (and some girls and women) can completely lose the respect of <u>some</u> of those present and even endure shaming, bullying, hazing, shunning...even worse: torture and murder.   I think you already know this.

I was just about to express my opinion that boys, more frequently than girls, when they leak tears or cry are called *crybaby*, but I decided out of curiosity to first check on the definition.   I am glad that I did.   This is what I found—crybaby: *a person, especially a child, who sheds tears frequently or readily; synonyms:* **sissy, mama's boy, wimp, wus**.   Yup, applied primarily to boys and men.   (I never have heard a girl or woman called any of those names.)

I also found this: *a person, especially a child, who cries readily for very little reason; a person who complains too much, usually in a whining manner.*   Although this definition doesn't specify boys and men it certainly reflects ignorance of discharge's value.   **Really, there is no such thing as *very little reason* or *complains too much* if tears are shed, but society does not know this which is why deprogramming ourselves and also helping others, especially boys and men, deprogram themselves is no easy task and probably never will be.**

Ironically, so powerful is our social conditioning to help young males learn to *control their emotions for their own good* that we adults, when in the company of a boy or teenager who begins to cry, can do the reverse of help even though we approve of emotional discharge.   We can compulsively shut this person down...with our facial expression, words (of comfort, sympathy, criticism, guidance and advice, or judgment), or actions (a hug, patting the shoulder, invitations to eat, etc.), or if this person is really young and unable to defend himself, with compulsive threats, slaps, and blows that we learned during our own childhoods are the appropriate responses to crying.   The list of potentially damaging responses to emotional discharge is far too long.

It is a fact: the harsher we were treated as children when we cried, the harsher we may be tempted, as adults, to treat children and young people.   Most of us, fortunately, manage to control our impulses because we are very determined to avoid doing to others what was done to us.

Now, do not assume that I believe girls have it easy.   No. Adults can react to their crying the very same way that they react to boys and young men.   However, violence is far less likely, in particular, violence that leads to torture or death.

All of our young people need to know that they not only have our permission to discharge emotion when they are in our company, they have, also, our encouragement to discharge emotion.   We need to be **VERY** clear about this since most behavior patterns are hard to change. Because programming to inhibit the stress-busting process of emotional discharge can, in some families, begin not long after birth, some young people need deprogramming as much or more than most of us who are adult.

So, working together, let's change beliefs and attitudes that are harmful rather than helpful.   We can do this!   I hope that the information you find in this book will help.

CHAPTER 60

WEALTHY $$$ WITH DEPRESSION/MOOD SWINGS

If you grew up in a wealthy family, especially if in a super wealthy family, and if while young you were extremely sensitive to peer and adult reactions to your natural emotionality, and if you were *corrected*, shamed, or scorned for crying, or were constantly distracted by your well-meaning parents, than you may have become a child genius at automatic self-distraction, which immediately placed you at risk of depression and mood swings, depending on your genetic inheritance.

You may have been placed at risk, also, of feeling constantly compelled to accumulate, accumulate nearly anything, and as you grew older there was the possibility that your focus of attention became the gradual accumulation of possessions and wealth since approval, recognition, and prestige likely followed.

If thoughts of wealth-accumulation automatically replaced awareness of stress/emotional distress you certainly couldn't discharge and bust stress. This invariably resulted in an increased focus on accumulating possessions and wealth as well as an increased risk of depression/mood swings.

You do not deserve that!

IF you see yourself here I hope you <u>will</u> seriously consider learning to practice skillful emotionality.   Recruit some family members or friends to participate.   That probably will not be easy to do as everyone you know has been programmed to ignore, discount, deny, and bury painful feelings and emotions.

Personally, I hope that you choose to become part of this most essential venture.   If you sometimes feel empty, lonely, lost, or confused (about anything) or if you have the strong suspicion that your true Self has been damaged or obliterated, you definitely will have the opportunity to rescue and restore that original, exuberant, creative Self while helping others do the same.

<u>That</u> is what you deserve!   AND!   If my suggestions are inadequate, seek out professional help soon if not now.

(Do reread Chapters 28 and Chapter 52, on obtaining the right kind of help.)

<u>(Please, for me, also read Chapter 63.)</u>

CHAPTER 61

AGAIN, OUR SOCIAL PROGRAMMING

EXPECT REPETITION! EXPECT REPETITION!

Frequently, we receive valuable information but are unable to make use of it because of our social conditioning. Is that happening to you right now? Are you still thinking, "This is crazy. Absurd. I don't believe any of this. I'm not going to make a fool of myself by crying when anyone can see me. I'm not going to cry even when I'm alone. Period. And this book is junk!"

If you think that, I can't possibly fault you. A reaction like that is normal. We all are strongly programmed to ignore information about the value of crying/emotional discharge. Some information is out there on the Internet (look for it). We simply need to take the information seriously—*crying with tears is good for us!!* ♥

So, in how many maliciously methodical ways were most of us so totally programmed to avoid the process that we now shudder and even react with horror at the idea of intentionally activating it? Picture a gigantic zero—there was no malicious programming.

As you probably know, soon after birth we became acutely aware of the behavior of those who interacted with

227

us or were merely present.   We listened for, and as sight developed, watched for, their eyes and eye movements, facial expressions, tones of voice, and body language. We were living perfect sensors for everything including, when we cried, signs of adult discomfort or disapproval.

Many of us who have relived early childhood experiences when we cried have learned that we were truly terrified of abandonment when our parents reacted negatively and this terror often made us cry harder, the reverse of what our parents wanted.   Ultimately, once we had gained greater control over our bodies, we stopped ourselves as quickly as possible if we started to cry .   Eventually, some of us learned not to cry at all, not at all!   (You?)

This programming process has always been simple: each generation of humans has very naturally conditioned its next generation to, *at the very least*, be extremely uncomfortable with emotional discharge.   There is no logic to this; it is learned and passed on, like prejudice and bigotry.   So, enough!

RETRAIN YOUR MARVELOUS BRAIN,
and I beg you,
HELP OTHERS TO DO THE SAME!

CHAPTER 62

DEPROGRAMMNG #3

Imagine saying this out loud or actually say this out loud:

MAYBE ALL THIS MAKES SENSE.

Imagine believing,

MY EMOTIONS AND EVERYONE ELSE'S EMOTIONS ARE ALWAYS IMPORTANT.

Imagine telling yourself,

NOTHING WILL STOP ME FROM LEARNING

ALL KINDS OF STRESS REDUCTION

PRACTICES.

Imagine believing and also telling yourself and someone you know,

CRYING WON'T KILL US.
IT WON'T KILL ME.
IT WILL EMPOWER US.
IT WILL EMPOWER ME.
IT WILL LIBERATE US.
IT WILL LIBERATE ME.

Or say this out loud,

I will become an expert at emotional discharge, like Pam.

You can do it!

CHAPTER 63

A WEE MORE REPETITION

Repetition, Repetition, Repetition

Growing up, we were happier *with* the discharge process than without it. We were more emotionally connected to ourselves and to those in our immediate environment, i.e., family, etc., which means we felt we belonged, we did not feel alone and isolated, we weren't *rocks* or *islands*. We were able to be and show our full selves rather than a *part* of ourselves. We did not have to pretend *everything is fine, I am fine, I don't need to share anything with you, I love having secrets about myself.*

For most of us, however, as we grew up the emotional discharge process gradually became a prisoner in the lockup of our minds and bodies. We became socially acceptable robots, unable to feel universal empathy and compassion. If we had any of those most human and desirable feelings, they were exclusive, limited to our *group*: family, friends, social or economic class, nation, etc.

Well, it's time to liberate this prisoner, this physiological process. We need this process because with it in our lives we treat ourselves and one another much more patiently and kindly, we are more flexible in our reactions to Life's demands, and we are less impulsive and compulsive. With the process in our lives we think more clearly, not only about our own welfare but the welfare of all lives here on Earth.

Now, you still may find all this good stuff impossible to believe. I understand that, but because I meditate (irregularly) and enjoy reading about the scientifically proved benefits of meditation, I am reminded that there was a time when the benefits of meditation were considered by many to be a product of gullibility and a good imagination. Not anymore. Science has proved it has value. The same will prove true for emotional discharge. But don't wait for science!! If you notice a gathering of tears and a painful thought,

trash your doubt and try crying it out.

CHAPTER 64

DEPROGRAMMING #4

If you were convinced by society and those people in your life that tears and crying represent weakness or imminent collapse, repetition is absolutely necessary.

Please, read the following words three times in succession. If you like, mouth them silently and really sense the movements of your tongue and lips. (Imagine that the words taste good. Yummmm. They do taste good, to your brain.)

TEARS ARE OKAY FOR ME.
CRYING IS OKAY.
I AM OKAY.

TEARS ARE OK FOR YOU.

CRYING IS OKAY.

YOU ARE OKAY.

Remember this: your beliefs (and attitudes and viewpoints) will determine whether or not you are able to:

- discharge at all.
- discharge as long as you need to.
- discharge as intensely as you need to.

Your beliefs (and attitudes and viewpoints) will also determine whether or not you obtain <u>full benefit</u> from your discharge.   I want you to be able to do that.

CHAPTER 65

MENSTRUAL CYCLES
AND MENOPAUSE

This may be the shortest chapter in the book. Come to think of it, I am confident that it will be.

We who are female know that during menses, due to hormonal changes, we can be **VERY** easily frustrated, irritated, and emotional. At these times we become less able to conceal and control our feelings and emotions and we become less able to ignore painful thoughts, whatever they might be. The good news: we are more likely to clearly see those things in our lives that produce stress.

Efforts to conceal-and-control add to stress. Therefore, it is beneficial to practice skillful emotionality when the impulse to do so arises...and to include additional stress reduction practices as much as possible, too.

Feel like crying over dishes or the computer keyboard or the steering wheel of your car, etc.? Do it while noticing the thoughts that flash through your mind! If you aren't alone, prepare those around you. Say, "I have to cry off some stress."

If your partner or husband or children, friends, or companions don't understand the value of emotional discharge, explain the value as best you can and/or give them this book.   Highlight or underline the pages you think most useful.

It is not a simple matter, retraining others.   It is most challenging, actually.   Please, for your sake, accept the challenge.   Don't let embarrassment or shame prevent you from activating the emotional discharge process and busting stress.   You are worth too much to let these programmed feelings rule your life.   If necessary, seek out a support group or therapist.

You   really   are   worth   it!

As for menopause, stressful time, too.   You know what to do, though!   Right?

(This wasn't the shortest chapter.)

CHAPTER 66

MEN WHO <u>REALLY CAN'T</u> *GET ENOUGH*

I am sorry, but what you read next is opinion, my opinion. I won't be quoting research papers on this problem though there has been a lot of research.   I have not interviewed professionals in any field of human nature, male sexual behavior, and human physiology although I would love to take the time to do so.   This is opinion, and if you happen to be a guy this is my opinion about you...<u>if</u> you never feel as though you *get enough*.

I have no doubt that you are doing the best you can to live a good, productive, and rewarding life.   Give yourself credit.   If you feel that you simply cannot obtain enough sexual satisfaction, please consider the possibility that you were born with the vulnerability to stress-induced depression/mood swings and have learned to reduce stress and elevate your mood, perhaps even to feel better about yourself and your life, with sexual activities.

Unless you are taking advantage of young people and adults through uninvited touching, harassing, abusing, intentional seduction, or intimidation, there is nothing wrong with using sexual activities to reduce stress and manage your moods, but if you have read the book this far you know that you are depriving yourself of a fuller life, closer and deeper genuine relationships, and the physiological and psychological benefits of emotional discharge.

You are a good person.   Please take the content of this book seriously and take action for your own sake, especially if those you love and care about encourage you to do so.   You deserve a life rich with love, meaning, and purpose.   I want you to have it.   Don't let unrecognized depression/mood swings stand in your way.   .

CHAPTER 67

DRUGS, ALCOHOL, AND OUR VULNERABILITIES

I don't think it is a secret that those who regularly drink too much or use illegal drugs are trying to feel better or not feel at all. If you do either or both, you may have inherited *the vulnerability*. If you have read this far and you suspect you are trying to avoid depression/mood swings, read again my words of encouragement for those who *cannot get enough*:

> You are a good person. Please take the content of this book seriously and take action for your own sake, especially if those you love and care about encourage you to do so. You deserve a life rich with love, meaning, and purpose. I want you to have it. Don't let unrecognized depression/mood swings stand in your way.

PART FIVE

BEING HIGH

CHAPTER 68

MOOD SWINGING <u>UP</u>

Are you wondering why I waited so long to introduce the subject of mood swings?   I certainly would have wondered why, I think.   I delayed because I wanted you to first be familiar with (1) the emotional discharge process and its stress-busting/invigorating function, (2) my successes practicing emotional discharge, (3) the practice of emotional discharge, itself, and (4) the practice I named *skillful emotionality*.   You now are ready for my take on mood swings, in particular, on moods that swing up, and on the use of emotional discharge.   (I hope we already understand and agree on the enormous value that emotional discharge possesses to help us bust stress.)

Before we get into my take on *getting high* (next chapter), let's see if we agree on this slightly reworded definition of mood swings that I found on the Internet.   I think it is pretty accurate and clear.

> Mood swings, which are relatively sudden variations in mood or emotional state, <u>are normal.</u> <u>They are harmful only when</u> feelings/emotions become *excessive, all-consuming,* and *interfere* with the demands of daily living.

The italicized words say it all.   What do you think?

So, in this section we are addressing the experience of being high (I don't like the term *manic*). If you swing high you know what it feels like. When we are high we can feel excited, elated, intense, awesomely energetic, powerful, 100% confident, and liberated both from the bonds of depression and the rigidities of culture. We can be super-creative and super-productive. We can lose sleep but not worry because we no longer seem to need much sleep.

What else? We also can suffer agitation, anxiety and panic, sleeplessness, and disabling exhaustion. We can take risks and make decisions that we later regret, often regret terribly. We can begin projects that actually make little sense or that are valuable but not attainable due to our mental/emotional state. Things can feel almost too exciting and too beautiful—too *anything*, actually. We can feel totally out of control and helpless to do anything about it.

That's being high. I've probably omitted far too many aspects of your experience. My apologies.

CHAPTER 69

MY TAKE ON GETTING HIGH

My perspective on the high-side of mood swings, on *getting high*, is not conventional. It is entirely based on my own experiences. I have not read a similar viewpoint, at least not yet. See what you think about it. Don't worry if you disagree with me, even find my interpretation and reasoning absurd. How you feel about my interpretation has no bearing on the fact that emotional discharge reliably busts stress.

I do not view *getting high* as the *manic* phase of a psychiatric disorder named *bipolar disorder*. I view it, instead, as a conditioned response to stress made possible by an inherited capacity to rapidly respond to stimuli.

How do we become conditioned? Good question. My answer: since we don't want to experience stress and/or emotional pain, and since our moods/emotions respond so quickly to any change in our thoughts or activities, we <u>learn to think certain thoughts and do certain things</u> <u>whenever we are **likely** to feel stress or emotional pain.</u> That is, we gradually learn to focus our attention on things that we like or that make us happy, become experts at identifying the thoughts, ideas, memories, images, activities, etc., that raise our spirits. Switching our attention to these mood-lifting thoughts, etc., becomes so automatic that eventually some of us don't even know when we are stressed or emotionally distressed and suffering.

Well-meaning individuals unwittingly provided the basic foundation for the expression of this genetic capacity. Those of us whose parents regularly and actively distracted us when we were upset (*here, have some pudding; let's go for a swim; let's visit Aunt Jean; look at this, sweetie*), who managed to get us to focus our attention on something other than what is stressing or upsetting us, thought they were helping us. They were not, but there was no way they could know this.

Those of us whose parents/caregivers verbally encouraged us to *think about something else* or *think positively* or *think about the advantages, not the disadvantages* increased the likelihood that we would learn to intentionally change our moods because the mood change *tool*, changing our thoughts, redirecting our focus of attention, was placed directly in our conscious minds by our parents or caregivers.

All of these parental efforts to (1) help us deal with stress and physical and emotional pain, and/or (2) help them deal with our behavior and emotionality, created and strengthened neural pathways of emotional distress/pain

244

avoidance. Not good. We never developed stress tolerance or emotional resilience.

Certainly, we who swing *up* can be very <u>lucky</u>: we are able to control our moods and energy levels simply by controlling our thoughts and focus of attention. For example, we can deliberately think proven mood-elevating thoughts and almost immediately enjoy a surge of energy and enthusiasm that can propel us out of bed or allow us to attend a function we would prefer to avoid. (Occasionally, I am now tempted to energize myself with thoughts but I don't dare do that; what if this reactivates that dangerous behavior pattern of swinging up?)

Certainly, we who swing *up* can be very <u>unlucky</u>, too. An unchanging pattern of intentional distraction will certainly prevent us from achieving self-awareness and self-knowledge (insight), and without both we may fail to improve situations and relationships, we may be unable to share the truth about how we feel with friends and loved ones because we simply cannot experience distressing emotions, and we may not seek help in a timely fashion or at all. <u>So, repeat after me:</u>

Absolutely and unequivocally, because self-awareness and self-knowledge are critical to my well-being, and because I am vulnerable to becoming "harmfully" high,

I will learn to recognize and gradually (or immediately) give up the practice of intentional mood manipulation.

There is nothing easy about eliminating our coping strategy—getting high. So what do we do? We learn to notice subtle impulses to (1) think mood-changing thoughts and (2) begin mood-changing activities. We learn, also, to remind ourselves that these impulses signal a need to bust stress.

Obviously, our major challenge-and-opportunity is to consciously gain control of this often automatic avoidance process. The next chapter contains some suggestions for doing that.

CHAPTER 70

USING EMOTIONAL DISCHARGE TO ELIMINATE "HARMFUL" MOOD SWINGS

You Can Identify Triggers

Very gradually, I learned, if magnificent Nature or anything else was almost too beautiful, painful, or meaningful, or if an idea was unbearably stimulating or upsetting, or if an experience was far too exciting, THIS indicated that I was under unrecognized stress and needed to discharge emotion; somewhere in my body and mind stress like a silent demon lurked and it was my job to discharge it when the time was right. (There are no such things as demons, of course, unless we refer to computer routines called *demons* or *daemons*.)

Each of us has the ability to become intellectually aware of at least a few of our *triggers*. One swift way to identify some of them is to generate a list of <u>potential</u> stressors. If you feel moved to do that, you can finish the following open-ended sentences with <u>as many different responses as come to your mind</u>. Get your pen, pencil, or keyboard ready Or turn on your voice recorder and dive in. Record your very first thoughts—

I FIND IT HARD TO...

I FIND IT CHALLENGING TO...

IT MAKES ME NERVOUS TO...

IT SCARES ME TO...

I FEEL TENSE WHEN...

I FEEL PRESSURE WHEN...

I GET UPSET WHEN...

I DON'T LIKE TO THINK ABOUT...

I DON'T LIKE TO REMEMBER...

Once we have a pretty clear idea as to what makes us feel tense, pressured, or upset, our mood-swing suspects are exposed and we can be on guard, prepared for anything. Personally, when I want to be aware of immediate stressors in my life I like to answer this question which is included in the list of attention-using skills:

WHAT'S DIFFICULT
OR HARD FOR ME RIGHT NOW?

You might ask yourself that question often so that you are aware of existing or potential sources of stress. You also might even invite a family member/friend to hear your response to that question and then, to respond to it, themselves. You could say, "Do you mind if I share with you what I'm finding hard right now? When I'm done, you could share with me something that you find hard. I hope you will."

"What's difficult or hard for me right now," might be a life-saving question for someone you care about.   They may have been struggling silently with life's demands until you came along with this invitation to share their personal Reality.

♥

What else can you do to identify potential mood-changing triggers?

You Can (Lovingly) Interrogate Yourself

You can tackle the problem of mood swings by answering the following questions and then planning to discharge emotion when your response to at least one of the following questions is, "Yes."

1. Do I feel high or depressed or suspect that I am?
2. Do I feel like crying?
3. Do I notice tension/pressure (stress and strain)?
4. Am I experiencing *any* painful feelings/emotions?
5. Do I feel physical distress or pain?
6. Am I finding it hard to think?
7. Do I feel confused or conflicted about anything?
8. Do I feel unusually foggy or sleepy?
9. Am I contemplating doing something unwise or at the very least unconstructive such as something that could make a situation worse or produce health problems?

249

10. Is *this* a trigger for my mood swings?
11. Do I recognize a behavior pattern for emotion-avoidance?
12. Am I finding it impossible to stop thinking about painful/upsetting *things*?
13. Am I finding it impossible to stop thinking about exciting *things*?
14. Do I feel inferior in any way, intellectually deficient, physically or emotionally weak, unattractive or undesirable, uncreative/blocked, or anything other than intelligent, creative, physically and emotionally strong, brave, and delightful to be with?
15. Are family/friends asking me if I am depressed or high?   We do get defensive here, don't we, so let's resolve to practice stating exactly how we feel and how we have been feeling.   Let's then be blunt and ask for some attention for emotional discharge.
16. Can I add any questions to this list?

YOU are wise and growing wiser with every burst of wet, messy tears!   Do not give up.

CHAPTER 71

LET'S LOOK AT POSITIVE THINKING, AFFIRMATIONS, AND COGNITIVE THERAPY

I do not know how many people primarily employ, and therefore depend on, the practices referred to in the chapter title, but I imagine it's in the millions. You may practice one or more of these stress-reducing, mood changing practices. That is why I now ask us to take a look at them. In the next chapter I discuss a concern.

Positive Thinking

Over the decades, positive thinking has enabled millions to forge ahead at certain times in their lives in spite of obstacles of all types. It's been called *learned optimism* and its outcome, generally, is a helpful (constructive), rather than harmful (destructive), change in attitude or expectation accompanied by a natural elevation of mood.

I just searched the Internet using "best books for positive thinking" and nearly toppled off my chair. Instead of being trampled by stampeding buffalo I was trampled by a herd of books. I am not going to list all of the book titles I spied, but *positive thinking* as a practical way to deal with stress has long had many proponents. It also has its opponents. On the Internet I found these books:
Bright-sided: How the Relentless Promotion of Positive

251

Thinking Has Undermined America, and, "*Smile or Die:
How Positive Thinking Fooled America and the World*."
Both books are by Barbara Ehrenreich, an American
author and political activist.   The book titles intrigue me.
You, too?

Without a doubt, positive thinking has stress-reduction
and mood elevation value.   However, I would never
recommend that anyone use it exclusively to raise their
energy level, their mood, and their expectations.   Those
of us vulnerable to becoming high should be extremely
cautious about the use of positive thinking...unless we
have achieved enough self-awareness and self-knowledge
to know when we need to discharge emotion and can do
so, as needed.   Remember, for those of us who get high,
stress and pain avoidance can be hugely hazardous.

Positive Affirmations

Positive affirmations is popular and useful as a
stress-reduction, mood changing practice.   If the website
still exists, you will find the following definition on the
Internet—https://www.powerofpositivity.com

**11 Powerful Affirmations to Help Treat
Depression and Anxiety.** *Affirmations are
positive declarations and self-scripts meant to mold
the subconscious into a more positive form.
Lately, this new-age practice is being hailed by*

practitioners and their patients as a potentially revolutionary practice.

Examples of affirmations include (all from the Internet):

1. I love myself unconditionally.
2. I am STRONG!
3. I find and enjoy the simple pleasures life is offering right now.
4. I am in control of my thoughts and my life.
5. My mood creates a physiological response in my body.   I m peaceful and positive.

To that list I would include what I say to myself when I need to:

1. I am doing the best I can right now.
2. I can do this.

Also, from the Internet,

http://www.essentiallifeskills.net by Z. Hereford:

Positive affirmations can be used to help you re-program your thought patterns and change the way you think and feel about things, about any things.   They are short positive statements that can help you focus on goals, get rid of negative, self-defeating beliefs, and program your subconscious mind.   Examples from Z. include:

1. I know, accept and am true to myself.
2. I believe in, trust and have confidence in myself.
3. I learn from my mistakes.
4. I know I can accomplish anything I set my mind to.
5. I forgive myself for not being perfect because I know I'm human.

Just like positive thinking, the practice of positive affirmations has proved to be useful.   There again, for the same reasons mentioned above, I would not recommend that positive affirmations be used exclusively.

Cognitive Therapy

Because both positive thinking and positive affirmations involve thought manipulation (or management), both have a little in common with the systematic, thought management psychotherapy, cognitive therapy, founded by Dr. Aaron Temkin Beck in the 1960's. He realized that those suffering from depression shared a common problem: over time they had developed automatic, false (unrealistic and exaggerated) negative beliefs and assumptions about themselves that depressed their moods, clouded their thinking, and affected their behavior.

So what is cognitive therapy?   I obtained from the Internet, at WebMD, the following information—

http://www.webmd.com/depression/features/cognitive-therapy

Cognitive therapy provides a mental tool kit that can be used to challenge negative thoughts...With cognitive therapy a person learns to recognize and correct negative automatic thoughts. Over time, the depressed person will be able to discover and correct deeply held but false beliefs that contribute to the depression.

Cognitive therapy posits that most problems have several parts. Those parts include:

1. *the problem as the person sees it.*
2. *the person's thoughts about the problem.*
3. *the person's emotions surrounding the problem.*
4. *the person's physical feelings at the time.*
5. *the person's actions before, during, and after the problem occurs.*

Cognitive therapists help their patients take each problem that arises apart so that they can identify and understand the viewpoints (beliefs, assumptions) about themselves, others, and the world that influence their moods and determine their behavior. Specific strategies are developed to correct unrealistic thinking and adopt more constructive ways of reacting to the demands of life.

Cognitive therapy has great value but it should not replace the practice of discharging emotion when there is stress or emotional distress.

CHAPTER 72

MY TAKE ON POSITIVE THINKING, AFFIRMATIONS, AND COGNITIVE THERAPY

Managing and manipulating our thoughts, attitudes, and viewpoints definitely can reduce stress and positively affect our moods and our behavior. All three practices referred to in the title are valuable for this. However, in my opinion, we don't want any of those strategies to <u>replace</u> the practice of emotional discharge. Hopefully, I have provided you with enough reasons to agree with me: none should replace emotional discharge. Don't we human beings need to re-sensitize ourselves to our personal experiences of reality as revealed to us by the emotions that we feel? Of course, we do, so let's not further our desensitization by encouraging the development of new patterns of emotion/memory avoidance.

Certainly, let's adopt new, more accurate, useful, even uplifting attitudes, beliefs, and viewpoints; let's identify and change inaccurate and self-defeating beliefs; let's deliberately tweak or extinguish unconstructive or harmful behaviors and behavior patterns and establish new more productive behavior patterns; let's reprogram our thinking. But! We also must experience our emotions. Am I suggesting that we discharge emotions every time emotions arise.   No!   I am saying we must always be able to feel them consciously and possess the ability to discharge them when they produce stress.

While searching for a brief yet useful definition of mood swings on the Internet I encountered instead, on a Goodreads site, the following statement by Louise L. Hay, motivational speaker, author, and publisher:

> *I don't fix problems.   I fix my thinking.   Then problems fix themselves.*

Fixing thinking implies the cognitive approach.   Here is the skillful emotionality approach.

I don't fix problems.   I don't fix my thinking.   I fix a harmful societal misapprehension that prevents me from liberally and eagerly accessing the emotional discharge process.   When I discharge emotion, solutions to problems appear and I fix those problems.

A Personal Story

Those of us who grew up in the 1950's were often told, "Look on the bright side," and "Things will work out for the best."   I suspect that some of us were conscientiously trained by our parents/caregivers to think positively.

When my mother died suddenly in 1991 due to multiple medical errors, in spite of myself I did consciously look for *bright sides* because she had told me to do that.   I found bright sides.   She would have been happiest about the money she was able to leave my brother and me.   She would have been relieved, also, to die relatively quickly. Definitely, positive thinking insulated me from the grief, horror, and rage that I was not at all prepared to experience at that time in my life.

Distraction played a major role in my survival, too. Because the nature of her death shocked and horrified me, I watched shocking and superbly presented Alfred Hitchcock movies such as, "Rope."   Because I was subconsciously feeling rage, I also watched, multiple times, three excellent sequels to PSYCHO which most people have never heard of.   I read three times in a row the excellent Bourne Trilogy by Robert Ludlum (THE BOURNE IDENTITY, THE BOURNE SUPREMACY, and THE BOURNE ULTIMATUM) and reread Robert Anson Heinlein's STRANGER IN A STRANGE LAND and STARSHIP TROOPERS.

Straight out of my subconscious I also wrote, with the help of a local police officer, an unpublished but copyrighted novel, SATURATION POINT.   Childhood emotional abuse, psychosis, motiveless murder, betrayal, wrongful death, and revenge were issues my brain examined for excellent reasons.

Despite my mom's death I also kept my job.   Thanks to the practice I managed stress as well as possible, discharging emotion at least once a week—though never over my mother's unnecessary death. (I did produce a detailed report which I delivered to the authorities.)

While writing the book that you now read I realized something important to me regarding my mom. She had good reason to believe that I would benefit from learning the practice of positive thinking—positive thinking had helped her wrench herself out of episodes of black dog depression.

Perhaps you can imagine how much I wish that I had been able to give my mom the emotional support that she deserved so that she could cry without shame or embarrassment whenever *the dog* approached. Had I been able to do that, the black dog would have become a runaway puppy, nipping at her heels one moment then gone, in time gone permanently.

I still use positive thinking at times. Wisely, I avoid all self-deceiving statements. My favorite: *It's okay to be upset. I can do it. It* could be anything.

CHAPTER 73

TWO TRUE TALES—MOOD SWINGING UP!

Let me begin with a sort of lighthearted experience of caffeine and (imagined) community.   The experience was not harmful and I hope that you find it somewhat entertaining.   Maybe you have had similar experiences, yourself.

SEARS, I LOVE YOU!

I hadn't been out of the state hospital for more than a few months when I decided to go to the local Sears Department Store at the mall.   Although I didn't realize it at the time, I tended to get high when I was in public places where I didn't know anyone: strangers would never expect me to appear successful and psychologically *together* so I felt more relaxed with them than with family and friends.

This particular day, once at the mall I had one cup of coffee with ten cups of sugar and then entered Sears.   I began wandering.

There was no warning!   Suddenly life was awesome because Sears made it awesome.   Every product that met my eyes was either exciting, fascinating, or gorgeous. The merchandise displays were brilliantly arranged, even artistic. The sales clerks were my kin and our varied relationships exhilarated me. We were family! We were the Sears family! I belonged here. I loved every sales clerk. I loved them all so much that I wanted to cry (what I actually needed to do because of ongoing stress). When I finally left the store I was exhausted.

Obviously, that was a super-memorable caffeine-and-stress-driven high. Probably, it was my very first experience with being high. (Before my two hospitalizations I had never been *high*. The word wasn't even in my vocabulary.)

Numerous similar experiences occurred during my first two years of recovery and I always remained totally clueless as to their actual nature, calling them *intensity periods* (rather than manic periods) in the journal that I kept. If anyone had asked, "Are you high," I would have been mystified. My wonderful psychiatrist certainly never used the word with me, but in his notes, which I obtained in 1976 or so, he wrote this: "Pam was in today. She was high, talking fast. She'll be back in the hospital soon."

Get ready for the more serious tale now, one where stress, not caffeine and stress, induced a high.

HOW I ESCAPED

Bookstores and coffee shops, those were the stimulating settings that flung me into the stratosphere mood-wise, and it was two bookstores and the supercharged increasingly complicated relationships that I gradually developed with their kind male owners, one of whom was married, which fueled the high that my observant and skilled doctor had referred to.

Was he right? Did I end up in the hospital as he predicted? No. I did not end up in the hospital. A few months after he wrote his observation, I moved back to my hometown an hour away with no no idea that I had been finding both relationships stressful.

It was a strange experience, not logical thinking, that kept me out of the hospital and ultimately determined my future trajectory. This is what happened. At that time I was a *tray girl* in the local hospital kitchen. Retrieving plates of cold luncheon food from the chilly cooler and stacking them on the shelves of rolling carts was one of my daily tasks. One particular day when I was in the cooler I reached into the shelving for a salad plate and heard a voice say, "It's time to go."

I was startled!! However, I didn't ask myself, "Did I say that?" Or, "Who said that?" Or, "*Go*? What does that mean?" Instead, I correctly interpreted what I heard and soon told my mom I would be eventually moving back home.

Did I ever wonder about the voice or if there was a reason why I decided to move? No. I was too emotionally fragile to question much of anything. At that time in my life self-interrogation on any serious matters was impossible.

I look at the event this way: emotionally I could not have handled any serious relationships so my brain, subconscious recognizing that a serious relationship could develop, in its wisdom spoke out, "It's time to go."

Impressive, huh, how the brain/mind tries to save our lives. I escaped without one clue that I truly was escaping . So, let's hear it for the brain, for the brilliant subconscious.

Thank you!

Good job! Really good job!

PART SIX

TALES OF DISCHARGE

CHAPTER 74

A REMEMBERED LOST OPPORTUNITY

It was the late 1940's. I was quite small, probably three feet tall. Wearing my little white cotton apron with the lavender flowers splashed all over it, I was standing, silent, in our brightly lighted kitchen looking up at my mother who was busy at the sink. I remember her turning toward me, smiling, and saying in a definitely loving voice, "Honey, are you mummy sick?" Nodding, I wrapped my arms around her legs and while she stroked my hair I buried my face in her own long yellow apron. After a few moments we separated.

I probably needed to cry. Most likely I had felt lonely and therefore sad. This must have been a seminal moment for me because I have never forgotten that incident. I recall experiencing a vague sick-like feeling but no physical sensation indicating a need to cry.

I believe this may have been one of the last moments when, at that particular stage of my development, had I cried and then continued to cry whenever I felt emotional pain, my vulnerability to depression/mood swings would have been reduced somewhat or even eliminated. After all, every time the emotional discharge process is used by the brain/body the neural networks are activated and the easy availability of the process is therefore maintained.

Had my mom automatically knelt down and held me while smiling, while wordlessly looking deeply into my eyes, would tears have begun to drip down my cheeks?   Might I have then bawled off some stress as well as some painful emotions that I felt but could not name?   Had she continued to hold me, her smiling eyes on mine, would that marvelous physiological process we call emotional discharge have continued unimpeded until I had cried off the stress of numerous hurts that neither of us recognized, as hurts?   Would I have then bounced off, full of zest?   I really don't know.   I will never find out.

CHAPTER 75

THERE WAS SOMEONE WHO CRIED BEFORE SHE LEFT FOR WORK

I told you that my mom suffered from black dog depression. It would hit her suddenly, the *world would turn black and there would be no hope*, and then it would clear up, it seemed to her, all by itself. I can imagine what dealing with my two hospitalizations must have been like for her. I imagine it was hell.

I told you that my mom tried to give me useful information. Well, I think she was always trying tell me it was okay and helpful, to cry.

She taught sixth grade at a time when each teacher taught all the subjects for her grade. She loved teaching and loved her students and like most teachers then and now had a great deal of homework to deal with nearly every night. Despite her workload, when I was in the state hospital in Vermont she drove three hours every Saturday to spend the day with me. She would bring pea soup, sandwiches, homemade desserts, and all kinds of other delicious things for a lunch that we would eat far away from the hospital in parks, beside streams, you name it.

During one of those visits she let me know that she would cry all the way back home. I will never forget her words: *I sound like an express train.* Once home, after all that crying, she did feel better. (I have no doubt that she also cried before she went to work. Imagine the loneliness.)

Sad to say, when I was in the hospital my mom's words about crying made no impression on me. I don't even know if I tried to comfort her. Being in my own depressed little world, it never occurred to me to comfort her and I never connected any dots, certainly not these: *I cried all the way home and felt better.*

While I was in the hospital my mom had no emotional support. Were there any support groups in 1968-69 for family members of those struggling with a *mental illness*? I don't know the answer to that question but I do know this: the Mental Health Association of Connecticut, formed in 1909 at the initiative of a mental health patient named Clifford Beers, began the family support group movement in Connecticut while I was still working there, perhaps sometime around 1977. (It was a few years before the National Alliance for the Mentally Ill began its own family support group movement in Connecticut.)

I will always be extremely sad that my mom dealt with my hospitalization alone, so please, if you are a family member or friend of someone struggling with depression/mood swings and any other mental health problem, don't let yourself go it alone. Attend family support group meetings. You can talk there. And cry! Make it safe for yourself and for everyone else, to cry.

Say, "I'm going to cry in a minute.   I really need to."
Then, cry.   For a minute or two.   No one will be alarmed;
it will be obvious that you know what you are doing!

There is one more thing that is important to me and
appropriate to add here:

PLEASE READ THIS!

While I was in the state hospital,
my mother and I cried together, but
only once.   We sat on the bed in a
small, cell-like room, and wept.

I have not forgotten that incident.
If we had realized how therapeutic
crying was we would have cried
together as often as possible.

We didn't need
permission; we needed
the knowledge that
crying busts stress and
heals.

PART SEVEN

MY BELIEFS

REPETITION REPETITION REPETITION

is
essential because the conditioning that we have
received and survived—
to ignore, discount, deny, and bury
emotions/information—
is so extremely powerful.

CHAPTER 76

LET'S HEAR IT FOR THE BEAUTIFUL BRAIN!!!

You and I are the recipients of a magnificent *living gift*. It is the brain. Usually, we take its presence in our lives for granted. We credit our parents and their genes (and our home environment, society, and culture) for how well or how poorly it functions for us. We assume that when it *fails* us there are logical, understandable reasons for this.

As societies we spend enormous amounts of energy and money researching remedies, solutions, and *cures* for its failure to meet our needs. For our existence and quality of life we depend on it—we all know this. But, big BUT, by depriving our brains free access to the emotional discharge process and its stress-busting, emotional pain reduction functions, this happens:

> we ignore, discount, deny, and bury valuable
> information that the brain has conscientiously (and
> continuously) gathered, analyzed, evaluated, and
> categorized for efficient retrieval. Our brains are
> designed to provide us with useful information but
> too often we don't want to be aware of or think
> about the information it has provided. We put all
> our energy into trying not to notice and think about
> what we observe, for example, what we see, what
> we hear, what we read, etc. In short, we don't

recognize and/or face reality and we force our brains to perform neural gymnastics so that we can remain unaware and ignorant.

Really, how much might we be screwing up this perfect instrument by forcing it to re-route all kinds of data?   What happens when neurons that should be involved in processes are underutilized or unused?   Could degeneration result?   Shouldn't we try to find out??

By constantly preventing the brain from activating its most effective maintenance and repair physiological process, we probably cause it, and the rest of our bodies, more harm than we can possibly imagine.   Our poor brains are literally handicapped in their ability to serve us well.

So, *let's hear it for the brain* and give it permission to be itself and *do its thing* when it needs to.   It desperately needs our support and cooperation!

YOUR BRAIN IS GOOD.

LOVE IT.

DON'T LEAVE IT!

You Must Begin to Love

and

Trust Your Brain

CHAPTER 77

DEPRESSION, THE WORLDWIDE EPIDEMIC

Stress-induced depression is the cause of a wide variety of reactions, or human responses. Most responses are not horrendous though some, like human and animal torture, murder including terrorism, and suicide, are. I believe that nearly everything we think or do which is counterproductive, harmful, or outright destructive begins with depression, with our brave and often fear-full efforts to deal with and endure depression. I believe, also, that once societies are well informed about the value of emotional discharge they will promote its use in a wide variety of ways and the incidence of depression will fall.

I am convinced that almost everything starts with depression, in infancy and childhood. This means that the most horrifying and observable human behaviors that harm humans and other forms of life, as well as the most subtle and least observable human behaviors (subtle emotional abuse and also neglect, for example), start with depression. This I believe based on my own experience with depression and with the behavior-and-thought patterns that developed in my childhood. I do not apologize for using a personal experience as a foundation for my beliefs since personal experiences are the basis of everything that we think, feel emotionally, and do.

I cannot imagine that there is any human who harms others who did not first endure a final, unbearable period of desperation and despair. I include here those who eventually decide to commit the most horrendous acts of violence .

CHAPTER 78

THIS I BELIEVE

As I write this book I am seventy two years old. Although I might have died at the age of twenty-three and taken any number of innocent people with me, instead I have lived long and prospered both psychologically and spiritually. Because of good fortune, I learned how to avoid the psychological curse of depression and harmful mood swings, and I want you to be as fortunate as I have been. So, please forgive me for a little more repetition.

Emotion is **not** unnecessary baggage, is **not** screwing us up and making us illogical, is **not** a waste of our precious time. We need emotion to successfully experience the entirety of Reality, and the process of emotional discharge enables us to use our emotions to reduce stress, heal emotional pain, and accurately process all the information that Reality provides.

Some of what used to be labeled junk DNA is considered *junk* no longer; a physiological process that some might label *junk* and others would like to junk will be proved to be the reverse of junk. It's our most natural, stress-busting process and we deserve to use it.

We are a socially interconnected and interlocked species capable of frightening destruction. We cannot escape ourselves or one another. We all sink or swim together.

So everyone, not only those of us who deal with the vulnerability of depression/mood swings, has to adopt a positive and therefore constructive attitude toward crying. If we all restore our ability to allow, as well as intentionally activate, *the process* as needed, our ability to face and deal wisely and compassionately with Reality will enable us to flourish.

Will everyone on our precious Planet Earth practice emotional discharge after learning about its immeasurable potential? Mmmm, I think you know the answer to that question. But humanity has to start somewhere; let it start with us! WE can help to lead the way.

We Must!

CHAPTER 79

WHY MY HEART BREAKS FOR PERFORMNG ARTISTS, PUBLIC FIGURES, AND ABSOLUTELY EVERYONE ELSE

Literally, it breaks my heart that so few are aware of the value of emotional discharge.   Do you know anyone familiar with its value?   When did you hear or read about this phenomenal process??   (Have you ever??)   This phenomenal natural physiological process that involves laughing and crying, which reduces stress/distress and helps us feel better because it produces endorphins and leucine enkephalin and does so much more for us, gets absolutely no air time and hardly any *print* time.

Imagine!   Our most natural stress-busting, information-integrating process, which provides us with stress, distress, and pain relief as well as insight and empathy so fundamental to wisdom, is spurned and scorned.   What kind of sense does *that* make?

I just searched the Internet for one thing and happened on something else, the following appropriate website: http://www.albany.edu/~drewa/health/practices.html

It is a website of the University at Albany.   On that particular web page the university was inviting people to list regular practices that they associate with maintaining or improving their health, whether or not a professional

recommended it or identified it as such.   Headings
included: Activities, Social Support, Mental Outlook, and
Emotional Regulation/Stress.   No list under any of those
headings included any reference either to allowing oneself
to cry (a common term is *release emotion*) when one felt
stressed, or, deliberately evoking emotion so that one
could cry (view a sad movie, etc.).   I consider this
tragic!!!!   **TRAGIC!**   No joke!

While waiting in supermarket checkout lines I always
study the covers of magazines and tabloids, searching for
titles related to health practices.   I never find articles
about crying.   I frequently foam at the mouth (not
obvious) due to frustration.

We learn about the trials and tragedies of celebrities, of
their children and spouses, and of public figures who,
stressed to the limit, suffering from unbearable fatigue,
anxiety/fear, and depression, begin to use drugs and
alcohol.   I won't list the names of all the good people who
have lost their health and their lives.   The exhaustion,
depressions, and/or mood swings that eventually got them
in trouble...or killed them...often might have been
prevented had they been able to reduce and/or eliminate
stress and distress on a regular basis using emotional
discharge along with their other health-enhancing
practices.   Sure, yoga, meditation, mindfulness, running,
lifting (weights), hanging upside down (inversion

therapy), spinning/cycling, martial arts, gaming, you name it, help. But!

Celebrities, public figures, and any of us, of course, can regularly exchange time with family, friends, associates, and even strangers and by agreement intentionally discharge emotion so that distress can't possibly build to the point of desperation and irrationality. During exchanges, no one has to reveal private information. Through use of one or more of the skills listed in this book emotions can be activated and discharged with minimal talk—nothing personal disclosed.

We have to face and accept the fact that lives are lost, fatal decisions are made (often on a grand and governmental/national scale) and humanity and all forms of life on our precious planet are at risk of extreme suffering as well as death and extinction. Why? Simply because cultural norms prevent most of us from crying when we are stressed and emotionally distressed and as a result we don't think clearly (though our non-logical thinking typically seems logical and wise).

Let's change those cultural norms with articles that tackle stigma and describe personal experiences with emotional discharge. We all learn from others' experiences when we read about others' experiences. We want readers to think, "Wow, that might work for me." Or, "Wow, after emotional discharge maybe I'll understand myself and other people a little better."

CHAPTER 80

STOP CRYING OR I'LL GIVE YOU SOMETHING TO CRY ABOUT

I am wondering if those words were ever spoken to you when you were crying. If they were, you felt instant fear or dread I am sure. You did not deserve to hear them but you did.

I am wondering if you ever said that to a child or young person. If your answer is *yes*, well, those words probably were said to you when you were young. So, you can forgive yourself for employing them but from now on...from now on...you know what I am saying. You really don't deserve to knowingly take on the burden of causing harm to another person by aiming those words at them. As you learn to bust stress you will no longer have any desire to use those words against anyone (they are truly threatening).

Were those words said to me? I really have no idea yet whether they were or not, but I certainly am familiar with them; I think those words are said more frequently and by more people than we can ever imagine. That is a tragedy.

Innocently, we humans continue to infect our young ones with a disease that can last a lifetime, a disease that actually can kill us all because it destroys our ability to feel empathy and universal love. The major symptoms of this disease are listed in this book. The major behavioral outcome is—**the inability to care enough about ourselves and Life to rescue ourselves and protect and defend Life (all living beings and all nonhuman forms of Life on Earth).**

If you wonder how I arrived here, at this topic right now, I will tell you: it is because I wanted to include in the book the words typed above in the title without having to change the page numbers as I already have changed them at least once and that really is enough. To avoid changing page numbers there was only one solution, to place the words, *stop crying or I'll give you something to cry about*, at the end of the book.

This might have been the shortest chapter in the book, but when I typed the words, *I'll give you something to cry about*, the chapter became a bit longer because I suddenly envisioned mountain scenes of our beautiful planet Earth, watched birds sail on air currents and whales lounge on ocean waves, felt grief and anger, and then thought, "We're really giving ourselves and future generations a great deal to cry about if we don't reclaim our ability to use the discharge process."

Truly, we need millions of people to:

1. rise up,

2. reject the insidious social programming that causes us to ignore, discount, deny, and bury our painful emotions, and
3. reclaim our natural emotionality.

We who are vulnerable to stress-induced depression/mood swings have such excellent reasons for embracing the emotional discharge process and ultimately understanding its inestimable value.   For our families and friends we can become models of its use.   We will be joining a new generation of humans worldwide who say, "Let's cry and laugh together so that we can feel merry and joyful and grateful together as we save everyone on Earth."

Now, please don't think you have to do anything other than reclaim your ability to use this process like a pro. You do not.   If the process works for you, the most helpful and loving thing you can do is spread the word.

Yes, spread the word, and let's change the title of our chapter to:

start crying and we'll give one another something to to feel joyful and triumphant about.

CHAPTER 81

LET'S *OUT* EMOTIONAL DISCHARGE NOW

Let's *out* the practice of allowing, as well as intentionally activating, emotional discharge—for our own sake, for everyone else's sake, and for the sake of all Life on Earth.

We can do that.

Let's out *IT, NOW!*.

Emotional Discharge

NOW

BIOGRAPHICAL SUMMARY

I grew up in the valley of beautiful Rutland, Vermont, USA, and graduated in 1966 from the University of Vermont with a B.S. in Education. A period of depression following the unexpected 1967 death of my father resulted in two psychiatric hospitalizations and the termination of my teaching career.

From 1969 - 1974 I held a variety of jobs before being hired as a secretary/admin. assistant to two non-profit organizations for 13 years each (the Mental Health Association of Connecticut and the Connecticut Pharmacists Association). Retired as of 2007, I am doing what I can to promote the ideas and type of practice that healed, energizes, and inspires me.

RECOMMENDED READING

FULL CATASTROPHE LIVING: Using the Wisdom of Your Body & Mind to Face Stress, Pain & Illness, by Jon Kabat-Zinn, 1990, Revised 2009

THE HUMAN SIDE OF HUMAN BEINGS, by Harvey Jackins, 1968.

THE PRIMAL SCREAM: Primal Therapy, the Cure for Neurosis, by Arthur Janov, Ph.D., 1970.

Made in the USA
Middletown, DE
14 April 2023

28831448R00176